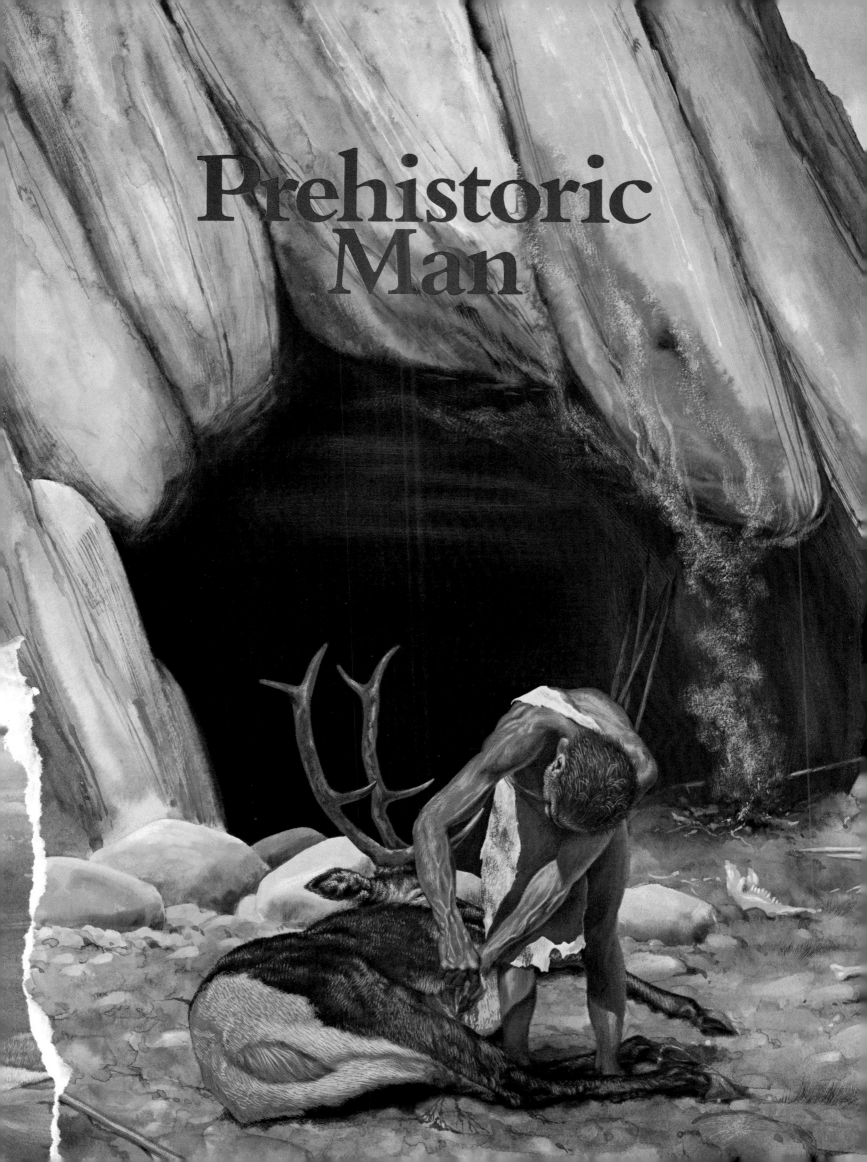

Prehistoric Man

Prehistoric Man

JOHN WAECHTER

The fascinating story
of man's evolution

octopus

First published in 1977 by
Octopus Books Limited
59 Grosvenor Street
London W1

© 1977 Octopus Books Limited

ISBN 0 7064 0605 2

Produced by Mandarin Publishers Limited
22a Westlands Road
Quarry Bay, Hong Kong

Printed in Hong Kong

Contents

Life Before Man

The development of animal life on Earth is fascinating enough, but that of Man is even more so. Unlike that of the animals the story of Man has two themes running through it: his physical development from the creatures which he was eventually to dominate, and his early attempts at invention and self-sufficiency. Man was an animal struggling to make good.

It is only recently that Man has gathered information regarding fossil animals and still more recently, little more than a hundred years ago, that he has accepted the idea of evolution.

The growth of the Natural Sciences, as with the other sciences, was handicapped by little systematic work being done before the eighteenth century, and a great deal of information having to be assembled before even the simplest of theories could be put forward with any hope of acceptance. The ideas underlying what we now refer to as the 'Theory of Evolution' are based on two major factors: a thorough understanding of the inter-relationship between existing plants and animals, and a considerable body of information regarding the creatures which preceded them and whose remains have survived in the fossil record.

The first man to attempt a serious classification of living things was the eighteenth-century Swedish naturalist Carl Linné, whose name is generally latinized into Linnaeus. Although some modifications have been made to Linnaeus's original classification, the basic principles which he devised are still in use and his method of naming individual animals allows one to place each creature into its proper place in the animal kingdom. The grouping of living animals by their physical characteristics was essential to the understanding of the fossil record which, since the middle of the eighteenth century, has produced increasing amounts of information.

Starting from the beginning of geological time, a period of some 4 600 million years, the soft-bodied single cell organisms which are the beginnings of life on this planet passed through simple forms of marine life to fishes, on through amphibians to the reptiles, and culminated in huge creatures such as the dinosaurs and their relatives which we always associate with fossil animals. From the early reptiles developed the birds and the mammals. Many forms came to a dead end in the process of change and development but others, by successfully adapting to changing conditions, evolved into the wide range of creatures of the present day.

By tracing the ancestry of any modern species, one can see that the various groups had common ancestors. For example, the dogs and wolves are both descended from a creature sharing many of their now distinctive features. The farther one goes back in time, the wider the range of dependents which each ancestor gives rise to, as with any family tree. The early forms of mammal which were on Earth nearly 200 000 000 years ago are the ancestors of all the present mammals.

In considering the development of Man there is no point in following the line right back to the beginning of life. It is sufficient for our purpose to take the group which he most resembles and to which the anatomists have assigned him, and take its members back to the point where they become distinguishable from the rest of the mammals.

From the very first systematic studies of the animal kingdom, it was clear that Man and the apes share many common features.

In fact the whole of the monkey and ape family was very similar and if Man was to be included anywhere in the animal kingdom his only possible place was with them.

The resemblance between Man and the apes is clear to us and was equally clear to the early exponents of the Theory of Evolution, which was becoming accepted by the middle part of the nineteenth century. But, whether this indicated a relationship or not, the early anatomists had a serious blind spot regarding Man's place in the animal kingdom. Man, according to the generally accepted opinion of the day, was the result of special creation, setting him apart from all other living things.

Darwin, though not himself the originator of the Theory of Evolution, produced the data which made the mechanics of the process comprehensible. He further clearly stated that Man, far from being the result of a special creation, had been subjected to the same evolutionary processes as any other animal, though during Darwin's lifetime little physical evidence was forthcoming about Man's immediate ancestors.

In some respects Darwin's ideas were misunderstood by some of his contemporaries. He never said, for example, that Man was descended from the apes, but that somewhere back in their ancestry Man and the apes had a common ancestor, an unspecialized creature with not much resemblance to either Man or ape. As one would expect these ideas of Man's place in Nature gave rise to a wide range of reactions, from derision to outrage, but gradually, with the exception of a small minority, they became the accepted theory as they are today.

The lack of fossil material in the nineteenth century, which made Darwin's ideas regarding Man's origin theoretical rather than practical, has been followed in the last 70 or 80 years by a mass of material bearing on Man's ancestry, some of which has shed light on the problem and some at present only confusion. Recent research has pushed us back into time ranges which would have been inconceivable to Darwin and his contemporaries.

The similarity between Man and the apes, to a lesser extent the monkeys, clearly indicates that it is with the family of primates that he belongs. This family contains, as well as the apes and monkeys, simpler groups such as the lemurs, bushbabies and tarsiers. One member of the primate group, the diminutive tree shrew, links the primates to some of the other animal families.

The first appearance of primates in any quantity occurs in the early part of the Tertiary, some 70 million years ago. This period has been called the Age of Mammals, since it is at this point that the dominance of the reptiles declined and the mammals came into prominence. The length of time covered by the Tertiary necessitates its being divided into four periods of unequal length. In the first, the Eocene, the primates are represented only by simple forms related to the later lemurs and tarsiers. As these have been found in North America, Europe and Asia, it is possible that this line may have started somewhat earlier.

By the second stage, the Oligocene, the Old and the New World monkeys had separated out into two major divisions with several clearly marked differences, such as variations in the number of teeth and the presence or absence of prehensile tails, such as those of the American spider monkeys. By the third stage, the Miocene, the ape stem was already established, probably having separated during the

CHART OF GEOLOGICAL TIME

CENOZOIC	QUATERNARY	RECENT	10,000 yrs	AGE OF MAN	Cro-Magnon
		Upper Pleistocene	150,000 yrs		Neanderthal
		Middle Pleistocene	1 m.yrs		Homo erectus
		Lower Pleistocene	4 m.yrs		A.robustus
	TERTIARY	Pliocene	14 m.yrs	AGE OF MAMMALS	Ramapithecus
		Miocene	35 m.yrs		
		Oligocene	45 m.yrs		
		Eocene	70 m.yrs		

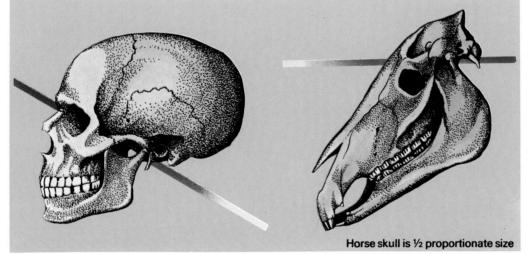

Horse skull is ½ proportionate size

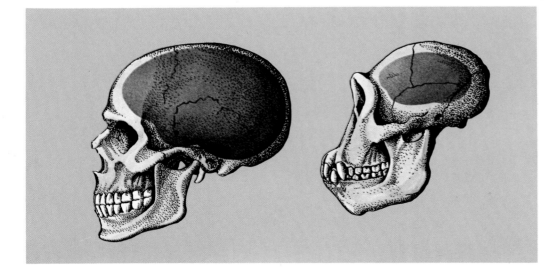

Left
Chart showing the geological stages of the last 70 million years, the period during which the primates and Man developed.

Centre left
A comparison of skulls of Man and horse. The main difference is the proportion of the brain to the face. In the horse the area occupied by the brain is extremely small: the teeth and nostrils occupying three-quarters of the skull. In Man the proportions are reversed, with the area of the brain far larger than the face. It must also be remembered that the brain size/body weight ratio in the horse is very small compared to that of Man.

Below left
A comparison between the skulls of Man and ape is only of limited value.

Both Man and the apes are on very specialized lines, but the farther one goes back to the point of departure of the ape and human, the less differences there tends to be. The first major difference between the two skulls is the very marked ridge across the top of the gorilla skull. This crest is mainly for the attachment of the muscles necessary to operate the very large jaws; the second obvious feature is the low vault of the skull and the marked slope of the ape forehead. One of the major developments in the human skull is the gradual increase in both the total size of the skull, and particularly in the important area behind the frontal bone. A further difference is the size of the brain itself in relation to the overall body bulk. The modern brain is on average around 1500 cc but that of the gorilla is only around 500 cc with a body weight over three times that of Man.

Oligocene from the main monkey line, together with what may have been fossil gibbons. The Miocene is particularly critical to the strictly human line for it seems that during this period the Man and ape (Hominid and Pongid) lines parted and went their separate ways. Somewhere at the point of separation was their common ancestor, the 'missing link' of popular fiction.

Several fossil primates dating from this critical stage have been found. Two, *Dryopithecus* and *Proconsul,* appear to belong to the anthropoid stem before Man and the apes separated, but there are two more which seem to belong to the early part of the human line. *Ramapithecus,* named after specimens originally found in India, was at first grouped with *Dryopithecus,* but re-examination of the original material has led several anatomists to move it over to the human side. Close to *Ramapithecus* are specimens from Kenya known as *Kenyapithecus,* one from the Miocene and one from the last stage of the Tertiary, the Pliocene.

The junction of the human and ape stem is the most critical, as well as the most difficult, area in human evolution. The amount of material available is extremely small and what there is is very fragmentary, generally only parts of jaws. A further complication is that at the point of divergence the differences between one group and another are small, and it is not until the human and ape lines have progressed some way along their lines of specialization that the differences become really clear.

Before coming to the final part of the jigsaw which makes up Man's family tree, it is necessary to consider in what way Man differs from his nearest modern relatives, the gorilla and chimpanzee. While the similarity between them is considerable, Man has traits which clearly separate him from his cousins; his upright posture and bi-pedal gait; hands with long thumbs, flexible enough to give precision as well as powered grip; feet with little toe mobility and thus not prehensile; a brain/body ratio far exceeding that of other animals; and, of course, speech. These major differences are reflected in different patterns of movement, different eating habits and brain development, all of which show in the appropriate parts of the skeleton but are less marked as one goes back towards the common ancestor. The sum of these special traits has been developed over a period of some 14 million years, but very gradually, so gradually in fact that there are stages where we are not certain whether we are proto-humans or humans, proto-apes or apes.

Although we have spoken of lines of descent, these in the genealogical sense are not available to us. In an ordinary family tree which is reasonably complete, each branch can be traced back to the founder of the family and the cross-relationship – brother, nephew or cousin – can be clearly seen by following the lines back to their common ancestor. If, however, instead of some hundred names all linked together one has only perhaps ten with no connecting lines and possibly no surnames, the likelihood of putting the individuals into their correct places becomes very speculative. Nevertheless we now have enough fossil material to give an overall picture of the emergence of Man, though some details may still be blurred.

Left
A cartoon of Charles Darwin published in 1871. This is one of a long series of cartoons showing prominent men of the day which included one of Thomas Huxley, an early supporter of Darwin's views; and also of Wilberforce, the eloquent Bishop of Oxford, rudely referred to as Soapy Sam. Wilberforce and Huxley clashed at the famous British Association meeting held at Oxford in 1860. Huxley supported the evolutionary ideas put forward by Darwin, while the Bishop defended the fundamentalist views shared by the majority of Victorians. Darwin himself took very little part in these controversies and was rather distressed at the furore to which his ideas had given rise, though throughout his life he never altered his views.

Right
Superficially the differences between Man and the apes appear to be considerable, especially in the stance, gait, teeth, shape of head, hands and feet, the size and development of the brain and the proportions of the limbs. In taking Man and the great apes together, we find that they appear to differ from each other far less than does each from other living creatures. There can also be no doubt that the gorilla and chimpanzee are Man's nearest relations, though they have undergone many differences in their evolutionary pattern.

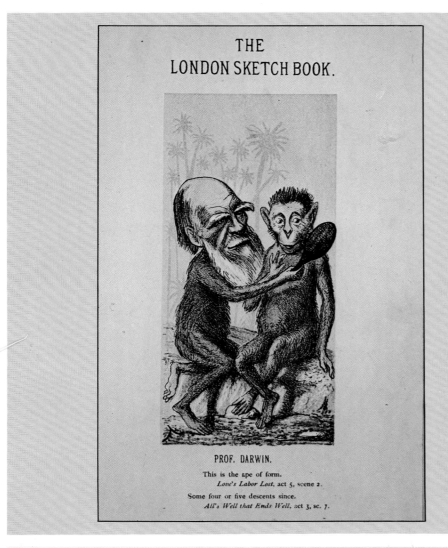

THE
LONDON SKETCH BOOK.

PROF. DARWIN.

This is the ape of form.
Love's Labor Lost, act 5, scene 2.

Some four or five descents since.
All's Well that Ends Well, act 3, sc. 7.

Left
This type of cartoon was very popular at the time of the initial controversies regarding human evolution. It panders to the general public's misconception as to what Darwin actually said. Nowhere in his book did Darwin say that Man was descended from the apes. What he did say was that Man had been subjected to the same evolutionary processes as all the other animals, and that he and the apes were only related in that both are descended from a common ancestor. Nevertheless, the error was more marketable to the cartoonist of the day than the truth.

Overleaf
Both the chimpanzee and gorilla use their hands a great deal for gathering and preparing food, for building simple tree nests or, as in this case, trying to scoop fish out of a pool. The chimpanzee in the wild has been observed to make use of simple tools, for example by peeling a stick and sticking it into a termites' nest. Chimpanzees are also known to pick up sticks to use as weapons.

Although the great apes are capable of walking upright, they are not very efficient at it, and their line of balance is such that they sway from side to side when walking. The gorillas frequently, when walking four-footed, use the knuckles of their hands to support their bodies. Their feet, unlike those of Man, are prehensile and, though not as efficient as their hands, are extremely useful in climbing and holding objects.

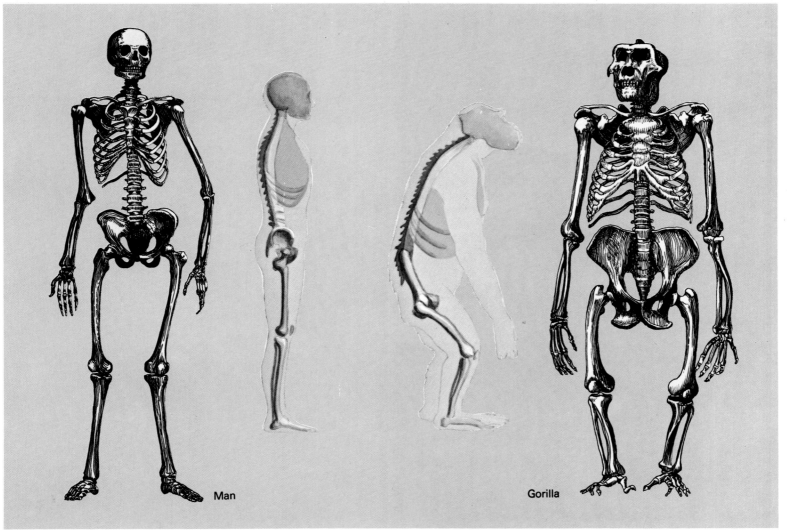

Man

Gorilla

Comparison of the teeth of gorilla, *Ramapithecus* (the earliest accepted member of the human line) and Man.

When considering differences in tooth structure and dental pattern between Man and ape, they appear to be most marked in the shape of the dental arcade. Each have the same number of teeth, but the geometry of the palate and lower jaw are vastly different. In the gorilla the cheek teeth in both lower and upper dentition are set in two parallel lines in a generally rectangular pattern. The human pattern is U-shaped with the lower jaw correspondingly wider. Most noticeable are the large canine teeth of the apes both in the upper and lower set. When the jaw is closed these two canines lie side-by-side, requiring cheek spaces which are missing in the human jaw. Between the teeth of modern Man and the great apes is a wide gap which is almost exactly filled by *Ramapithecus,* but in general his teeth are nearer the human pattern.

Below right
One of the hand-axes found at Hoxne in Suffolk by John Frere in 1897.

These were recognized by Frere as being something far more significant than simply human artifacts. To use his own words 'the situation in which these weapons were found may tempt us to refer them to a very remote period indeed; even beyond that of the present world'.

This observation was not taken up at the time and it was nearly half a century later that similar tools were attributed to an age which corresponded to their real antiquity. It is interesting to note that Frere used the phrase 'beyond that of the present world'. In this respect he was following the biblical narrative, and implying that these tools were made before the flood – i.e. when the historical slate was wiped clear and humanity started afresh with Noah and his family.

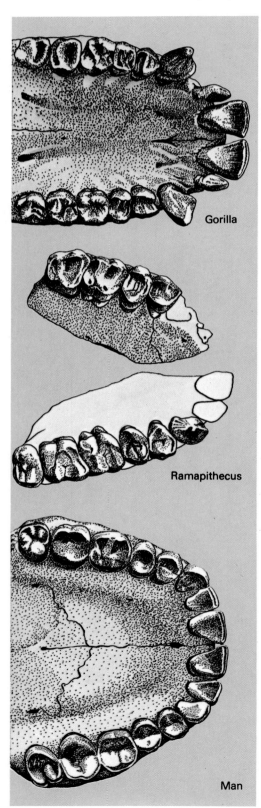

Gorilla

Ramapithecus

Man

All primates have prehensile feet, unlike Man. The long soles and toes enable primates to gain a firm grip of tree branches. Moreover, several primate species have evolved extremely efficient hands and, in certain instances, they appear to approach the dexterity normally associated only with Man.

One of the great assets developed very early on by Man was the dexterity of his hand, and the twin development of this and his brain are very closely related. It was not until the hand became free of locomotory function that it could evolve into its present form, a development which did not occur until Man was walking fully upright.

All the primates have a prehensile hand to some degree and most have a prehensile foot as well, but the human hand gains in efficiency by having an opposable thumb, which means a thumb long enough to touch the tips of each finger. This ability to bring thumb and finger together allows objects to be held and used by the tips of the fingers and thumb alone. This is the difference

between the precision grip and the power grip in which the object is held by wrapping the entire hand around it. While much of the stone-work of early Man could have been done by the power grip alone, for the finer work, particularly the developing craftsmanship and early art, a precision grip was essential.

A *Ramapithecus* family breaking up animal bones to extract the marrow and gathering fruit off the bushes. The bones were most likely the result of scavenging as it seems very unlikely that these creatures would have been able to catch game of any size. The tools used for breaking the bones were not specially made for this purpose and anything of sufficient size and weight would have been suitable.

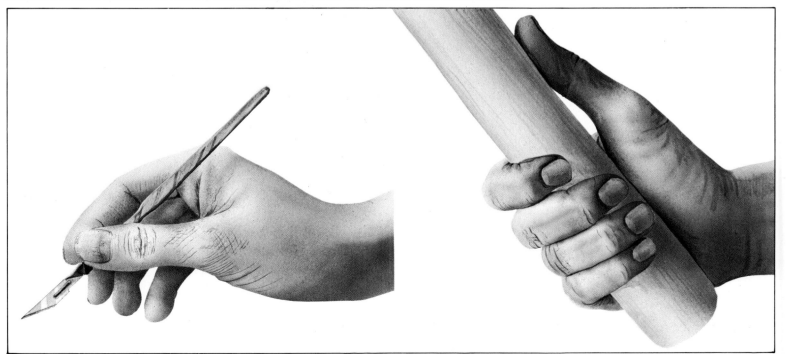

Dating Techniques

Our knowledge of the physical and cultural development of Man is based on a mass of information acquired over nearly two hundred years of excavation. The history of the unveiling of Man's past is also the history of archaeology as a science. The transition from the preserve of the week-end amateur digger to the highly complex discipline of today has been a long road; many mistakes have been made, much evidence has been lost through bad excavation and strong support has been given to many misconceptions. These have been the teething troubles of a young science which has had to overcome many difficulties, including forgeries and well-planned attempts to deceive.

If asked for a definition of the aims of archaeology, one would be justified in saying that they are total reconstruction within a framework of time. These aims are never likely to be fully realized. Excavation, the main method of archaeological research, has obvious limitations. A well-conducted excavation can provide a great deal of essential information: cultural patterns and development, changes of climate and data regarding the environment generally, lists of the animals hunted, the seasons during which the site was occupied, the diseases from which the population suffered, and much more. There are, however, aspects which have no written records, as is the case throughout most of Man's past, and cut us off from much of the abstract areas of early culture. Some facets of human culture, such as social structure, religion and oral tradition, will probably always be a closed book. Nevertheless a vast amount of material has painstakingly been amassed.

In addition to the rapidly increasing information regarding early culture and environments, as well as the physical development of Man, the new evidence of Man's early ancestry, and more particularly the greatly increased time ranges with which we are now dealing, has made archaeological research over the last few years very exciting.

Ever since the famous date of 4004 B.C. for the Creation suggested by Archbishop Usser in the seventeenth century, archaeologists have been looking for some form of clock which would accurately measure the span of Man's development. Until comparatively recently only inspired guesses as to the date of any event, either archaeological or geological, were possible and the time relationship was in any case too broad to be very meaningful. The date of 4004 B.C. has today been pushed back to an extent which would have astonished the early pioneers of archaeology.

In archaeological terms time can be seen in two ways, relative and absolute. Relative chronology is concerned with fitting episodes into their correct position in the geological sequence. Two different sites which are associated with the same geological feature are said to be of the same relative age within the duration of the feature which connects them, a time slot which may cover several thousand years.

In relation to the total span of geological time, now considered as being about 4 600 million years, the primates became a separate group only 70 million years ago and Man diverged from the ape stem only some 5 million years ago. In following Man's story, we are thus only really concerned with the later stages of geological time.

The four Tertiary stages of the Cenozoic–the Eocene, Oligocene,

Miocene and Pliocene–were followed by the fifth major stage, the Pleistocene–part of the Quaternary, which lasted some 5 million years and finished about 10 000 years ago. It was during the latter part of this period that most of Man's physical, and much of his cultural, progress took place, and it is here that we can see him becoming not only human but also the pioneer of human culture. The full significance of this progress can only be grasped if we understand the nature of his contest with the physical world and the time taken to achieve even the smallest advance.

The Pleistocene is by far the best sub-divided of all the geological periods. The initial breakdown is into Lower, Middle and Upper periods, based largely on well-marked changes in the animal life, some older forms dying out and new ones appearing. Although there are differences in the species represented in various parts of the world, the same basic stages can be seen in all the continents.

The finer sub-divisions are based largely on changes of climate. Throughout the Pleistocene there were peaks of extreme cold, ice ages or glacials, which alternated with warmer periods or interglacials. There were four main cold phases and three warm phases. The glacials are further sub-divided by smaller oscillations or interstadials, two in the first glacial, two in the second, three in the third and four in the fourth, all these divisions occurring in the last million years. These stages can be broken down into even smaller units and detailed studies of the soils which make up archaeological deposits have shown that it is possible to get a very good idea of the climatic conditions under which they were laid down. Even more sensitive is the analysis of pollen. The pollen grains which are carried in the wind are, in certain circumstances, indestructible, and it is possible from a soil sample to obtain a very clear picture of the plants which were growing at the time, the trees in particular. This in turn tells us the type of climate, and long pollen sequences can provide very accurate climatic curves.

As well as the direct effects of glacials on the climate, there were also very useful side effects. The sea level dropped during the peak of the cold phase when vast amounts of water were locked up in the ice sheets which covered much of the northern hemisphere. With the return of warm conditions in the interglacials, this water returned to the sea and the level rose again. The bed of the sea has gradually dropped over the last million years and the old shore lines with the remains of their beaches can be seen in many places on cliffs. Since we know which glacial belongs to which high sea level, it is often possible to relate an archaeological site on or near a beach to its correct position in the glacial/interglacial sequence. Similar evidence can be provided by the old terraces of rivers which, like the sea, responded to the alternating warm and cold conditions.

Although relative chronology has served archaeologists well for many years and is becoming even more precise, the idea of absolute time scales obviously has a greater appeal, particularly when we are trying to date sites in different parts of the world since using relative chronology alone is not sufficiently accurate.

Before the Second World War various methods for calculating accurate time scales were being pioneered. One, which has now been in use for some time, is based on the theory of solar radiation. The radiation from the sun has varied greatly over the last million years and it has been claimed that these changes were the cause of the glacials. It was also claimed that the changes of radiation could

Left
Cartoon showing the excavation of a burial mound or barrow in England during the early nineteenth century. Such excavations, usually week-end affairs, were not very scientific; not only were few, if any, records kept but much of the contents was eventually dispersed. It was not until the end of the century that excavations by modern standards were carried out.

Below left
This hand-axe was found in London at the end of the seventeenth century. Close by were the remains of an elephant. The hand-axe was attributed to an ancient Briton and the elephant to the Emperor Claudius. In fact the hand-axe is around 200 000 years old and the elephant was hunted by its maker on the banks of the Thames.

Overleaf
Stonehenge, a prehistoric monument in Wiltshire, is undoubtedly the best-known ancient monument in Britain. First accurately surveyed during the seventeenth century, it was attributed to the Druids whose temple it was supposed to have been. The monument is, in fact, of more than one period. The original circle is Neolithic, around 3 000 B.C. and the main ring of standing stones is Bronze Age. There are a number of these stone circles known in Britain and France, but this is by far the most impressive. Various suggestions have been put forward to explain its function, including that of an astronomical observatory.

be dated and thus provide dates for the glacials to which they gave rise. The calculations from the radiation evidence suggested that the Pleistocene began about 600 000 years ago and lasted until about 25 000 years ago, a far shorter period of time than more modern methods have indicated.

The real breakthrough in absolute dating came as a spin-off from atomic physics. This was Carbon 14, the best known of the radiometric methods of dating. In simple terms the principle behind Carbon 14 is that all living organisms acquire the Carbon 14 isotope from the atmosphere during their life. On death the Carbon 14 begins to decay at a known rate, so that the age of a sample can be determined from the amount of Carbon 14 remaining when it is excavated. Naturally there is a limit as to how far back one can date, since there is a point where there is no longer enough Carbon 14 left to measure. At present it is possible to obtain dates to about 50 000 years ago, but the possibility of error increases the farther back one goes. The most suitable materials for Carbon 14 are charcoal, bone and shell, but the samples have to be collected with great care. In the early stages of the use of this method many errors were made, largely through the researchers not understanding the effects of contamination. The packing material used to wrap the samples often contained a high rate of carbon of its own, tree roots introduced modern carbon into archaeological deposits, and water with modern amounts of carbon could have seeped through the ground. These problems are now being overcome, however, and the method is proving extremely useful.

In view of the length of the Pleistocene, the 50 000 years coverage of Carbon 14 provides dates for only a very small part of the total time span involved. It was obvious that other methods were necessary to cover the earlier periods if any degree of precision was to be achieved in dating archaeological events widely spaced geographically.

A technique which has gone a long way towards providing dates for the earlier periods is one known as potassium/argon, K^{40}/Ar^{40}, developed since the Second World War. This is based on much the same principle as Carbon 14, but involves the decay of potassium 40

into the gas argon, a process which like Carbon 14 takes place at a
known rate. The value of potasium/argon is that it provides dates
far beyond the range of Carbon 14 and can date back several
million years. There is, however, still a snag: the accuracy of
potassium/argon decreases as one reaches the younger dates, so that
by about 300 000 years the readings are no longer reliable. This
leaves a gap of about 250 000 years between the younger
potassium/argon dates and the oldest Carbon 14 dates. Physicists
are constantly working on this problem and new techniques are
currently being developed which are beginning to fill this gap.

Two techniques, one developed in Scandinavia and the other in
America, come under the heading of absolute chronology even
though they are not radiometric. The first, called varve analysis, is
based on the principle that the retreating Scandinavian ice sheet
deposited fine sediments in the lakes at the time of the annual
summer melt. The thickness of each varve depended on the
particular summer and a succession of hot or cool summers would
leave characteristic patterns of varves. If the section in a particular
lake was not complete, it could be matched up with longer sections
elsewhere. By matching up sections across Scandinavia from north
to south, it has been possible to follow and date the retreat of the
ice of the last glaciation.

The second technique, tree ring analysis or dendorchronology, is
based on the same principle as varves, although in this case it is the
annual growth of tree rings which provides the clock. Like the
varves, variations in temperature are reflected in the form of the
annual ring and all trees in the same area will have a very similar
ring pattern since they have been affected by the same conditions.
By matching the rings of trees of different ages it becomes possible
to establish a long sequence of ring patterns, into which any piece
of timber which was growing at any time during the tree ring
sequence can be dated. At present it is possible to date timbers back
for several hundred years and in America the technique has proved
successful in dating the timber houses of pre-Columbian Indians.

An extremely useful development of tree ring analysis is that it
can be used to check the younger Carbon 14 dates. The rings of the
American brissel pine, a very long-lived tree, has provided a long
sequence of dates. Parts of these trees whose dates are known have
been carbonized and subjected to Carbon 14 dating, thus providing
a very accurate assessment of the percentage of error with Carbon
14. So far it is not possible to take the tree ring dates back
anywhere near the full range of Carbon 14, but they can be used to
check dates to about 3–4 000 years B.C. and attempts are being made
to calculate the errors covering the full range.

Playing an increasing part in modern dating, either to check
other methods or to fill time gaps, are more techniques based, like
Carbon 14 and potassium/argon, on some form of radiometric
calculation.

For some time attempts have been made to make use of deep-sea
cores, provided either by geological sampling or exploration for oil.
The upper part of the ocean bed is made up of fine silts which have
been washed in and have settled on the bottom, and thousands of
generations of small creatures have also left their skeletons and shells
on the sea bed. These small creatures are very sensitive to changes
of temperature, and cannot live in conditions which do not suit
them perfectly. By identifying the warmth- and cold-tolerant
species represented in a deep-sea sample, the temperature of any part
of the core can be arrived at with considerable accuracy. Climatic
curves similar to those of the glacials and interglacials can be plotted
from the longer cores, and it is reasonable to suppose that the two
curves are related. The value of these cores is not only that they
provide complementary climatic curves which act as a double
check; it is also becoming possible to date them, by the radiometric
method known as thorium/uranium, where the uranium content of
the shells changes at a known rate into thorium. In theory these
thorium/uranium dates should fill the gap between Carbon 14 and
potassium/argon, but it is not always very clear which part of the
climatic curves from the sea core is being dated as many of the deep
sea cores are, for various reasons, incomplete.

As well as supplying some of the dates vital to archaeological
research, the information provided by the various methods of
relative chronology also provide the data on which our knowledge
of prehistoric environments is based. The uses of the two dating
techniques, relative and absolute, will become apparent as we
discuss the various periods in human development.

Over millions of years rocks have been forming one above the other, some from old marine sediments, some from volcanoes and others from mud. During the formation of each rock strata, the remains of creatures living at the time became incorporated in the rocks and have become part of the geological record. In the beginning the living creatures were very simple becoming gradually more complex until towards the end Man made his appearance.

Top right
Excavating an elephant's vertebra in river gravels in the lower Thames at Swanscombe, England, which date from around 250 000 years ago. In addition to the animal bones there were various simple tools made out of flint pebbles from the gravel. As well as being the locations of bones and tools of prehistoric Man, sites like these can also provide a great deal of information regarding conditions at the time. We know from the fossil remains of animals roughly what the climate was like, in this case much like Britain today, and this is confirmed by pollen grains. Some of these have been picked out of the teeth of elephants and rhinoceros.

Below right
Swanscombe is regarded as the richest Palaeolithic site in Britain. Now preserved as an ancient monument, Swanscombe is composed of a 30-metre (100ft) gravel terrace divided into two major phases representing different periods of river development. The upper level is associated with the Swanscombe skull and the lower level with a flake industry. Recent excavations of the lower level have revealed the presence of bones from a wide variety of animals, including bear and elephant. The lower part of the section shown is made up of river gravels and above are fine marsh deposits containing animal bones and stone tools completely undisturbed.

Not to scale

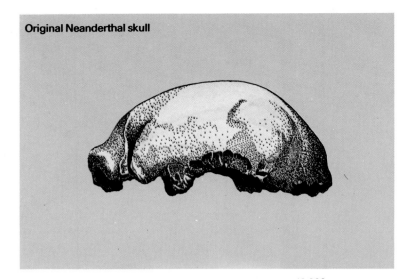

Left
This shows the original skull cap from the quarry at Neanderthal in Germany found in 1856, three years before the publication of Darwin's *The Origin of Species*. The skull consisted of no more than the top and part of the brow ridges yet it was, nevertheless, clearly very primitive in appearance. As there was no means of dating it (since no archaeological material was found with it), few anatomists would accept it as being a human ancestor, and most dismissed it as being the skull of an idiot.

Right
Chart shows the development of the primates during the last 70 million years–the Cenozoic era. The first stage, the Eocene, saw the primates already established and by the second stage, the Oligocene, the apes and monkeys evolved along separate stems. In the Miocene, ape and Man separated, with *Ramapithecus* being the founder-member of the human line. The lower Pleistocene saw the advent of *Australopithecus*, 1470 and possibly early members of *Homo erectus*. The Middle Pleistocene is the main period of *Homo erectus* followed in the Upper Pleistocene by Neanderthal Man and finally by modern Man.

Opposite top
This photograph taken in Alaska shows the front of a glacier moving down a valley. It is interesting to note how close the trees are to the ice. During the Last Glaciation in Europe, from about 70 000 – 10 000 years ago, Man occupied most of the ice-free areas and probably hunted right up to the very edge of the ice front.

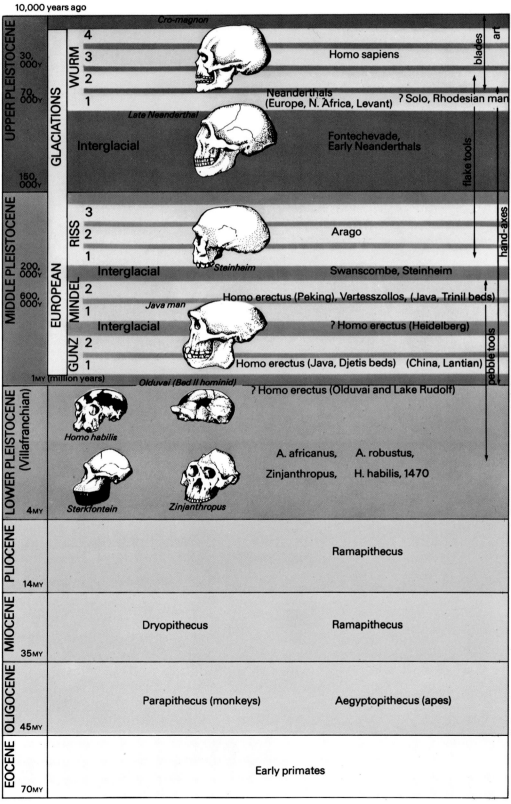

10,000 years ago

UPPER PLEISTOCENE	GLACIATIONS	WURM	4	Cro-magnon
			3	Homo sapiens
			2	
			1	Neanderthals (Europe, N. Africa, Levant) ? Solo, Rhodesian man
		Interglacial		Late Neanderthal — Fontechevade, Early Neanderthals
MIDDLE PLEISTOCENE	EUROPEAN	RISS	3	Arago
			2	
			1	
		Interglacial		Steinheim — Swanscombe, Steinheim
		MINDEL	2	Homo erectus (Peking), Vertesszollos, (Java, Trinil beds)
			1	Java man
		Interglacial		? Homo erectus (Heidelberg)
		GUNZ	2	
			1	Homo erectus (Java, Djetis beds) (China, Lantian)
LOWER PLEISTOCENE (Villafranchian)				Olduvai (Bed II hominid) ? Homo erectus (Olduvai and Lake Rudolf)
				Homo habilis — Sterkfontein — Zinjanthropus — A. africanus, A. robustus, Zinjanthropus, H. habilis, 1470
PLIOCENE				Ramapithecus
MIOCENE				Dryopithecus Ramapithecus
OLIGOCENE				Parapithecus (monkeys) Aegyptopithecus (apes)
EOCENE				Early primates

blades — art

flake tools

hand-axes

pebble tools

30,000Y
70,000Y
150,000Y
200,000Y
600,000Y
1MY (million years)
4MY
14MY
35MY
45MY
70MY

SPREAD OF ICE
OVER EUROPE

Left
During the glacial periods in Europe, the glaciers spread out from the mountains into the plains, and there was a huge ice sheet centred on what is now Scandinavia. The second major European glacier covered much of north Germany and all of the British Isles down to the Thames Valley. This shows the approximate ice coverage of Europe during the second or Mindel Glaciation, around 600 000–400 000 years ago. The map, based on Europe as it is now, does not include land exposed by the major drop in sea-levels which in some cases provided land wedges for prehistoric Man where none now exist. The rise in sea level has been universal and has covered much of the evidence of Man's existence on the sea-shore.

Right

In addition to being indicators of climate, groups of animals also provide information about which geological period the site fits. The illustration shows part of the lineage of the elephants. In the Pleistocene of Europe, the southern elephant only occurs in the early part, associated with a special form of rhinoceros. The southern elephant is ancestor to both the straight-tusked elephant and the mammoth, with an intermediate form in the middle of the Pleistocene. If, for example, a site contains southern elephant then it is no later than the early part of the Pleistocene, while more advanced forms indicate later periods.

Below left

Carbon laboratory, where archaeological finds are dated scientifically. Carbon 14 dating is based on the principle that, since all living organisms absorb the radioactive Carbon 14 isotope during their lifetimes and stop doing so at death, the date of death can be measured from the amount of Carbon 14 still left in the remains. The carbon disintegrates at a steady rate and it is this rate which provides us with a basis for calculating how long ago the organism died.

Below right

A section through an American sequoia tree. Although the annual growth rings cannot be clearly seen, the red lines indicate 50-year intervals. The time range covered by this tree is from about 550 A.D. to Darwin's publication of *The Origin of Species* in 1859. Any sequoia growing during this period will have tree rings which fall into this pattern.

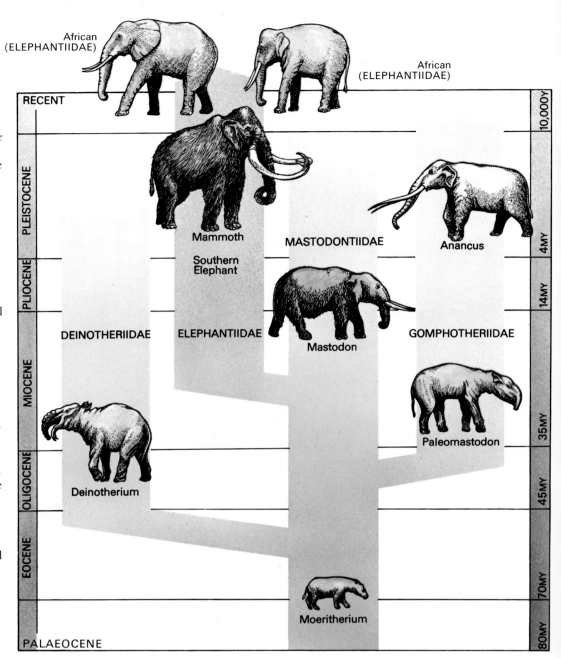

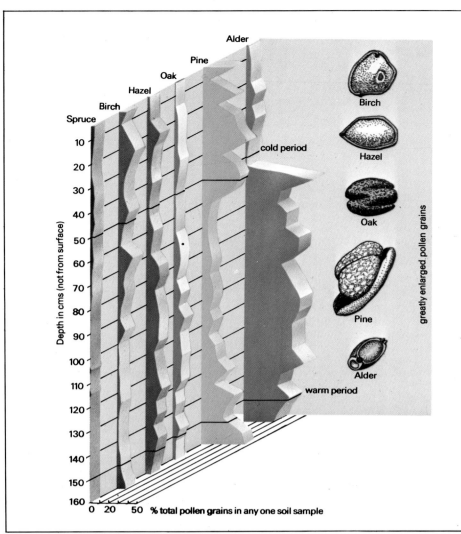

Left

This diagram shows how tree pollen has been increasingly used to indicate climatic conditions. In a cold climate conifers (e.g. pine) thrive and deciduous trees (e.g. alders) decrease resulting in a higher percentage of pollen from the former type. The reverse happens in a warm climate. Pollen grains are virtually indestructible and by comparing the various types it can be established whether warm or cool conditions prevailed at any given time.

Below left

The diagram shows how the pattern of one set of tree rings can be added on to the rings of an older tree. The date of cutting of tree trunks can be established with considerable accuracy, and it is thus also possible to date additions or alterations to a building.

Below right

Drawing of a section through a deep-sea core drilled from the sea bed.

The part shown may represent the deposition of several thousand years. The climate can be ascertained from the minute sea creatures whose remains form most of the sediment, some being tolerant of warm and some of cold water. It is also possible to obtain radiometric dates from these cores, thus dating climatic changes known elsewhere.

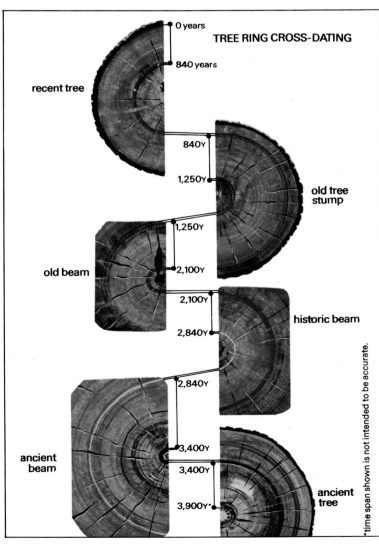

TREE RING CROSS-DATING

recent tree — 0 years, 840 years

old tree stump

840Y
1,250Y
1,250Y

old beam

2,100Y
2,100Y

historic beam

2,840Y
2,840Y

ancient beam

3,400Y
3,400Y
3,900Y

ancient tree

*time span shown is not intended to be accurate.

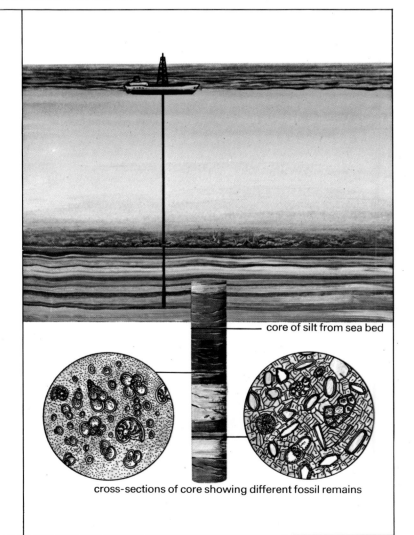

core of silt from sea bed

cross-sections of core showing different fossil remains

Man in the Making

The point at which the ape and the human stems separated appears to have taken place at least in the Miocene and probably in the preceding Oligocene periods, as both groups seem to be clearly defined by this time.

The Dryopithecines (see first chapter) stand without doubt on the line leading to the great apes and thus lie outside our story. Before leaving the Dryopithecines, however, it is worth considering them in more detail as they appear to represent creatures very close to our common ancestor.

The first member of the group was discovered in France as far back as 1856, and was the first of the fossil apes to be scientifically examined. Since then various members of this family have come to light in other parts of Europe, India, Pakistan and as far east as China, and more recently they have been found in East Africa.

Like most of the early fossil primates, no complete skeleton has been found and we are largely dependent on a few jaw fragments and isolated teeth for our information. The most complete skull, that of *Proconsul,* from the island of Rusinga in Lake Victoria, is so far the best specimen available and in addition there were enough limb bones found with it to provide us with some idea of what these creatures looked like.

In size they were probably midway between the modern chimpanzee and gorilla and the evidence of some limb bones suggests that they spent at least some of their time in forest environments, since the shoulder seems to have been adapted for swinging and the teeth are primarily for fruit-eating.

The other group contemporary with *Dryopithecus,* and for some time considered as belonging to the same family, is *Ramapithecus* (see first chapter). The original specimen came from the fossiliferous deposits of the Siwalik Hills in north India, an area which has in the past produced a mass of fossil material. Christened after the god Rama, *Ramapithecus* is the first recognizable candidate for the position of Man's direct ancestor; he represents the first step along a road which has been the most dramatic in the history of the world.

The position held by *Ramapithecus* might suggest that he is more impressive than he actually is; in fact the difference between him and the Dryopithecine is mainly a matter of difference in the form and arrangement of the teeth, the only parts which have survived. The teeth of *Ramapithecus* differ in both size and wear, and the remains of parts of the upper jaw show that the angle of the face is much flatter than in any of the apes. If one saw the two groups alive and together, however, it would probably be difficult to recognize that they were in fact evolving along two entirely different lines.

Ramapithecus, like *Dryopithecus,* has a wide distribution and is found in India, Turkey, Greece and East Africa. Of particular importance are the fragments of *Ramapithecus* found at the late Miocene site at Fort Ternan in Kenya. These pieces, consisting mainly of jaw fragments, were originally named *Kenyapithecus wickeri* by Louis Leakey, their finder. Recent re-examination, however, has shown that they do not differ to any extent from the *Ramapithecus* group and the Fort Ternan material is now included in the *Ramapithecus* family. Two other important pieces of information came from Fort Ternan: a potassium/argon date of around 14 million years, a figure near the junction of the Miocene and Pliocene, and also clear evidence that many of the associated animal bones were broken open by stones for the extraction of marrow. Was *Ramapithecus,* therefore, the first tool-user?

Tool-use has been observed among other creatures, for example when the Egyptian vulture breaks ostrich eggs by picking up stones with its beak and hammering on the shells, and of course there is the well-known trick of picking termites out of their nest with a stick which has been observed in chimpanzees.

The cause or causes which led to the divergence of Man and ape will probably never be known with complete certainty. Nor will we ever be really certain as to the stimuli which triggered off the mental and physical changes which have taken place over the last 14 million years. But it has been suggested that we acquired the foundation of our human traits when our ancestors first moved from the protection of the forest to the hostile conditions of the open savannah, forcing the small defenceless hominids to live not only by their wits, but to develop both body and mind as a means of survival.

The evidence is that the environment of *Ramapithecus* both in India and Africa was still largely forest, but apparently bordering open parkland, conditions which would have made a halfway stage towards open country.

Between *Ramapithecus* and the next recognizable stage of human development there is a considerable time gap. The latest *Ramapithecus* appears to date from the early part of the Pliocene, somewhere around 10 million years; our next sight of Man is not until between 5 and 4 million years, leaving a long period from which as yet we have no information.

It is from the beginning of the next geological period, the Pleistocene, that we have discovered in the last few years more human fossils than came to light in the previous hundred years—material that is more recognizably associated with modern Man than with *Ramapithecus.*

To understand the part played by these new finds it is necessary to examine them in the order in which they were found rather than in chronological sequence, otherwise the picture becomes rather confusing and the inter-relationships difficult to follow.

The first member of what is now called the Australopithecine was found in 1925 in a limestone quarry at Taung in South Africa. The Taung child consisted of a skull with the face, upper and lower jaws almost intact, and all the teeth present. Although most of the back and sides of the skull are missing, there is an almost complete cast of the brain which clearly indicates the overall shape of the head. The teeth are those of a complete milk set with the first permanent molars beginning to erupt, suggesting an age of about six years.

Raymond Dart, who first described the Taung skull, christened it *Australopithecus africanus,* the 'southern ape from Africa'. In spite of this name, Dart maintained from the beginning that it represented an early form of Man, a view which at first did not command general acceptance. Had Taung remained the only representative of the Australopithecines the controversy might have continued longer than it did, but the child was soon to be joined by a number of adults, also from South Africa.

Robert Broom, a colleague and early supporter of Dart's ideas, started investigations in limestone quarries similar to those at Taung and in a very short time found a mass of material clearly belonging

to the same group as the Taung child. In all Broom and his colleagues obtained material from three sites, Sterkfontein, Kromdrai and Swartkrans, all south-west of Pretoria.

The value of these new sites is that not only did they provide a great deal of additional material, but much of it was that of adults, so that the features which are poorly represented in the juvenile at Taung can be seen fully developed in the mature specimens.

The finds from Broom's three sites are not of one population but of two with quite marked differences, sufficient to place them into two distinct species. The first, based on an almost complete skull from Sterkfontein, is definitely that of an adult version of the Taung child with the same well-rounded skull and the same general face profile.

A further bonus from Sterkfontein was the find of a number of bones other than those of the skull, including enough of the pelvis to make a reconstruction possible. Putting together the evidence from the long bones and the pelvis, it is clear that the woman of Sterkfontein, for female she clearly is, walked upright, though probably not quite as efficiently as modern Man.

The second group of individuals from Broom's caves came from Swartkrans and Kromdrai. The best specimen, the almost complete skull from Swartkrans, is a typical representative of the group. These creatures are much more robust than those from Sterkfontein and Taung and also bigger. The adults have very large teeth and correspondingly large jaws. These large jaws led to the formation of

a ridge along the top of the skull to accommodate the muscles necessary for chewing, a feature shared with the gorilla. The very impressive jaws are attested by an almost complete specimen from Swartkrans which, though not belonging to the Swartkrans skull, fitted it reasonably well.

Further finds by Dart in the cave at Makapan limeworks, also in South Africa, have produced more material comparable to that from Sterkfontein, including another almost complete skull.

Both the Sterkfontein and Swartkrans populations, in spite of their differences, are classified under the name *Australopithecus,* the name Dart originally gave them. But they are separated into two distinct species: *Australopithecus africanus* for the lightly-built gracile type from Sterkfontein and Makapan, and *Australopithecus robustus* for the larger group from Swartkrans and Kromdrai.

The next major find belonging to this period of human development came from East Africa. Olduvai Gorge, in the eastern part of the Serengeti plain in Tanzania, is probably the richest hominid site in the world, and has been investigated for many years by the Leakey family.

The site, or rather sites, are situated in a gorge about 90 metres (300 ft) deep, cut by water through a series of old lake deposits and volcanic dust filling a deep depression. The 90 metres (300 ft) of deposit covers a time range of nearly 2 million years, and throughout this period the shores of the old lake provided suitable camping places for a wide range of hunter-gatherers of more than

27

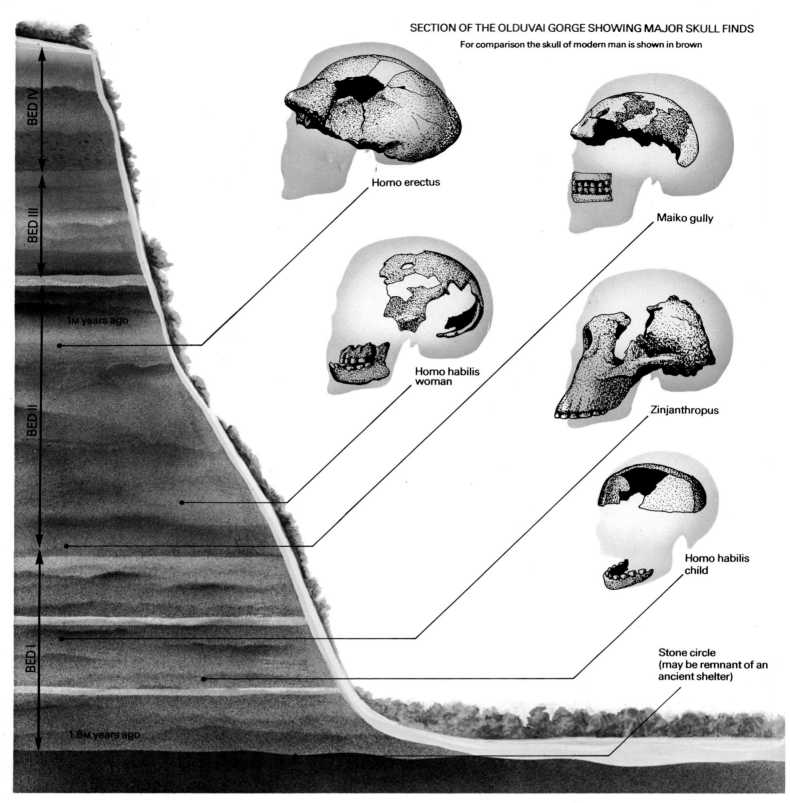

SECTION OF THE OLDUVAI GORGE SHOWING MAJOR SKULL FINDS
For comparison the skull of modern man is shown in brown

BED IV

BED III

1M years ago

BED II

BED I

1.8M years ago

Homo erectus

Maiko gully

Homo habilis woman

Zinjanthropus

Homo habilis child

Stone circle
(may be remnant of an
ancient shelter)

Previous page
View across Olduvai Gorge, Tanzania.
This is one of the most important fossil Man
sites in the world. The Gorge, nearly 90
metres (300 ft.) deep, is made up of old lake
sediments and volcanic ash from the volcano
in the background. The earliest occupation,
around 1·8 million years ago, was of early
hominids living on the shores of a lake and
making very simple stone tools with which
they cut up the carcases of game.

The figure in the foreground is Louis
Leakey who with his wife Mary investigated
the sites for over 40 years.

Above
This section shows the principal layers at
Olduvai Gorge. Bed I and the lower part of
Bed II contain the living floors of *Homo
habilis,* and from the same horizons came
Zinjanthropus. The upper part of Bed II
contains similar tools to the lower part but
they are more developed. At the top of Bed
II were found the first hand-axes and
remains of *Homo erectus.* Beds III and IV
have produced more developed hand-axes.

one human type, each roaming the area in groups.

This long geological sequence has been divided into four main parts, or beds. Bed I, the oldest, contains the remains of small camp sites originally on the margins of the lake and characterized by a scatter of broken animal bones and simple stone tools. For many years there was no indication as to the occupiers of these camps, but in 1959 the Leakeys came across fragments of a skull, which when reconstructed proved to be almost complete.

Louis Leakey named this new find *Zinjanthropus boisei*, the generic name being taken from an old term for East Africa. Zinj, as he is generally called, is a very robust individual with large teeth and, like Swartkrans, has a ridge along the top of his head to accommodate his enormous chewing muscles. He seems to be the earliest known hominid tool-maker.

Although no jaw was found with Zinj, an almost complete one of the same age was later found at Peninj near Lake Natron. This fits him exactly and shows the same massiveness that characterized *Australopithecus robustus* from Swartkrans.

Unlike the hominids from South Africa, Zinj was found in the middle of what was clearly a living floor, covered with animal bones and small tools made from pebbles into simple chopping tools. In view of this association, it was assumed that the camp site belonged to him and that the bones and tools were the results of his activities. Further excavation at the site has thrown considerable doubt on this idea.

About 50 cm. (20 in.) below the Zinj living floor, and thus older, came the remains of another human type who appeared to be more advanced than Zinj. *Homo habilis*, the 'handy man' as Leakey called him, was represented by part of the skull of a child with an almost complete lower jaw, and a foot and other bones of an adult.

The child, whose age is uncertain except that it already had its permanent teeth, had a brain capacity of about 100 cc more than Zinj, who was of course an adult; in addition the bones of the child's skull are much thinner than those of his slightly more primitive neighbour.

Both Zinj and *Homo habilis*, who are roughly contemporary, occur towards the base of Bed I and have a potassium/argon date of about 1·7–1·9 million years. The upper part of Bed I passes into Bed II without any break in the deposition, and both contain the same range of animals. Roughly halfway up Bed II there is an obvious break and a very clear change of fauna. This means that there is a break in the sequence and a time gap. How long the gap is between the two parts of Bed II is not known, but dates of about 1 million years old for the upper part of Bed II have been suggested. Both Zinj and *Homo habilis* continue into the upper part of Bed II and thus occupied Olduvai for nearly a million years.

The names originally given to Zinj and *Homo habilis* imply that they are sufficiently different from the Australopithecines from the south to warrant them being placed in a separate genera. The differences between Zinj and the robust form, *Australopithecus robustus*, are very small and Zinj is now included along with the Australopithecines under the specific name *boisei*. The placing of *Homo habilis* is not quite so simple; some anatomists also include him with the Australopithecines but others still consider that he could remain in a separate group.

Still further north, in Kenya and Ethiopia, hominid material is being found at an incredible rate, and the dates obtained are far greater than those from the base of Bed I at Olduvai. In Kenya work has been going on for a number of years under the direction of Richard Leakey, son of Mary and Louis, on the eastern side of Lake Rudolf, or Turkana as it is now called. The deposits in this area are in some ways similar to those at Olduvai, a mixture of lake sediments and volcanic ash, the latter being particularly important as it is from the volcanic beds that the potassium/argon dates are obtained.

Again, as at Olduvai, the fossil material is generally found eroding out of the sides of gullies cut by water in the soft deposits, and it is this erosion which has led not only to the discovery of the hominids but also to the camp sites associated with them.

It is still too early to understand the full significance of this new material, but it is clear that there are at least two groups present at Lake Rudolf. The first appears to resemble *Australopithecus boisei*, but the second, referred to only by its field number as 1470, is a much bigger-brained individual with a capacity estimated at about 800 cc, much greater than any of the Australopithecines and greater

than any *Homo habilis* discovered so far.

Further north the River Omo drains into the northern part of Lake Rudolf and rises in the Ethiopian uplands. Both the Americans and French have been working in this area for many years and have found a great deal of early hominid material within the same range as the main Australopithecine groups, and more is emerging from the eastern provinces of Ethiopia.

So far only the skeletal material has been referred to, but both Lake Rudolf and the Omo river have produced clear evidence of tool-making which seems to go back at least as far as 2·4 million years, nearly a million years earlier than the tools from the earliest levels at Olduvai.

Taking the African finds as a whole, and trying to see the relationships between the various groups and their place in the pattern of human development, presents tremendous problems. When the original Australopithecines were found, they were dated to the early part of the Middle Pleistocene, about 600 000 years old. In view of the estimated date for the Asian *Homo erectus* of about 500 000 years, it seemed that the African material was far too late to have been in the direct human line, and the Australopithecines were consequently relegated to the position of branches which died out. The discovery first of *Homo habilis* and later 1470 seemed to confirm that the Australopithecines were indeed off the direct human line of ascent, and that if *Homo habilis* is also an Australopithecine then only *Ramapithecus* and 1470 are the immediate predecessors of *Homo erectus*.

Recent finds from eastern Ethiopia and the site of Laetolil, not far from Olduvai, suggest that there are hominids at least 3 million years old which are more developed than any of the Australopithecines, but it remains a possibility that *Ramapithecus* or something very like him was ancestral to both the Australopithecines and Man. Whatever the nuances of relationship between the various groups during the period 3–1 million years ago, some of them at least represent stages through which Man has passed and thus demand some consideration as to their possible way of life.

All of the hominid or near-hominids around during this period were capable of walking upright, though probably none of them, including the most advanced, were as efficient bipeds as ourselves. At least some were tool-makers as well as tool-users. There is evidence that, though food-gathering probably provided most of their food, they certainly, judging from the bones found associated with many of them, had access to meat. Although *Australopithecus robustus* seems to have lived largely on a vegetable diet, that of *Australopithecus africanus* was more variable.

The early tool kits, like those from the base of Olduvai and the earlier East African sites, are made up of two components, the small chopping tools and the very sharp flakes resulting from their manufacture. Thus these early men would have been able to disjoint game and cut the meat from the bone, and the sharp flakes could have served for shaping wood. Whether they hunted in the accepted sense or got their meat by scavenging will be impossible to prove, but there is no reason to believe that they were less capable than, for example, the hunting dogs. In addition they would have been adept at catching the young and the weak, driving the bigger animals into swamps or laying ambushes at waterholes, and driving off predators from their prey.

Of their social structure we know nothing, of course, but one can envisage small family bands living largely on fruits and berries with the addition of small creatures such as lizards, snakes, tortoises and birds' eggs, and meat from the bigger animals forming a useful bonus. However they may have obtained their meat, the evidence from the camp sites shows that they were very proficient at cutting up even animals as large as elephants. Sometimes our early ancestor was not quite so successful as a hunter and himself seems to have fallen a victim—one of the Australopithecines from South Africa has two holes in the back of his skull which exactly fit the canine teeth of a leopard. It also seems that the majority of the Australopithecines were not inhabitants of the sites but the remains of prey dragged in by large animals.

One possible side-light on Australopithecines is the estimates of their age at death. Few of them lived more than 18 years, with the maximum 40. This suggests that such a low death figure would have left many orphaned juveniles and there must have been a social organization sufficiently complex to cope with them.

Right
This is one of the best preserved of the *Australopithecus africanus* skulls and bones found by Broom in a cave at Sterkfontein near Johannesburg, embedded in limestone. This skull is probably that of a female and is an adult of the species of which the child from Taung belonged. The brain capacity is about 480 cc, within the range of a gorilla, but the Australopithecines were very much smaller. These creatures from Sterkfontein are more lightly built than those from Kromdrai and Swartkrans and, judging from their teeth, were mixed feeders.

Right
Australopithecus robustus is one of the rugged Australopithecines first found at Swartkrans and Krondrai in S. Africa. They were bigger with more massive skulls and jaws and were vegetarians. This specimen from Lake Rudolf clearly shows the large face and heavy brow ridges. Although contemporary with *A. africanus* the differences in the skull are due mainly to diet.

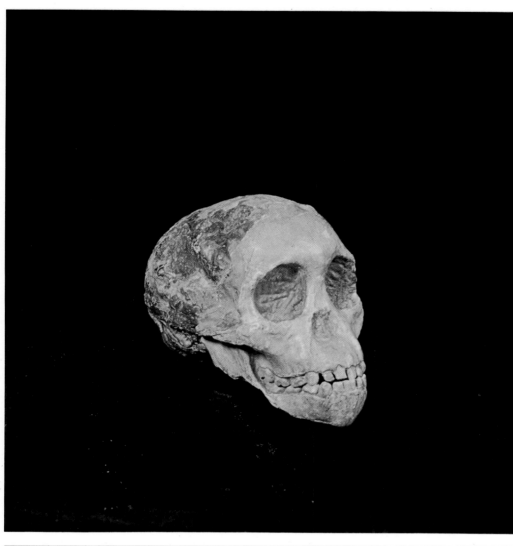

Left and below left
This child's skull from Taung (*left*) was the first member of the Australopithecines to be recognized. The left-hand side of the skull is missing but the overall shape can be seen and *below left* is the skull of a young chimpanzee for comparison. Although the general outlines of the Taung child are similar to the chimpanzee's, from the viewpoint of the different pattern of its teeth the Taung child is clearly not on the ape stem.

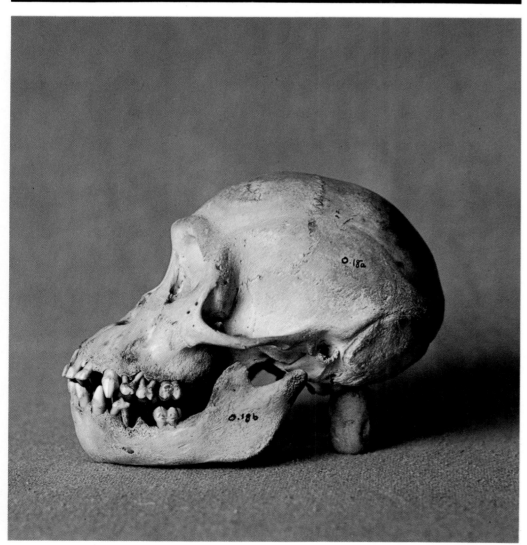

Right
Zinjanthropus or Nutcracker Man was the first early hominid to be found in Bed I at Olduvai by the Leakeys. This type is clearly related to the robust Australopithecines from S. Africa but is placed in a different species. Found on a living floor together with various stone tools, he was originally thought to have been the first tool-maker at Olduvai, but there is another slightly older hominid, *Homo habilis,* who seems to be a little more developed and was probably the tool-maker. The jaw shown came from a site not far away of the same age and fits reasonably well.

Below
The site in the lower part of Bed I at Olduvai where *Zinjanthropus* and *Homo habilis* were found.

The concrete blocks mark the *Zinjanthropus* level and *habilis* came about 50 cm. lower. Both horizons are over 1·5 million years old.

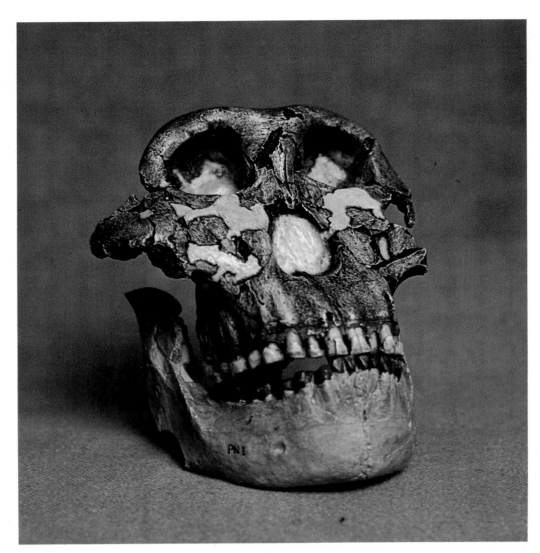

A selection of stone tools which were discovered in the lower levels at Olduvai. The two on the left are small chopping tools made in black basalt, and the one on the right, a rough hand-axe from the upper part of Bed II. The pebble choppers are known from sites around Lake Rudolf and these date back to about 2·4 million, so there is nearly a million years with no change in tool-type. In addition to the choppers, the flakes detached during their manufacture could be used as small cutting tools.

Below left
A general view of the Omo area, Ethiopia. Like the Lake Rudolf sites, the fossil bones and stone tools are found eroding out of the sides of the gullies. Hundreds of human fossils have been lost by this erosion, but without it none of the hominids would ever have been found. Much of the material from Olduvai came to light in the same way, but by excavating the sides of the gullies where its fossils were found the living sites came to light.

1470 Man, found at Lake Rudolf, is probably
the most important African hominid type so
far found. In both brain capacity (800 cc)
and general shape the skull seems to be
superior to any of the Australopithecine
skull types found in the same area at roughly
the same time, over 2 million years ago.

Although not directly associated with
1470, there are a number of sites in the area
which have produced stone tools very like
those from the bottom of Bed I at Olduvai,
where they were found together with
remains of *Zinjanthropus* and *Homo habilis*. It
is suggested, though still not proved, that the
tools from Lake Rudolf were made by 1470.

The conditions in which 1470 was found
are typical of the discoveries of many of the
hominids from East Africa. Very small
pieces of the skull were seen eroding out of
the side of a gulley. Weeks of careful sieving
eventually produced a mass of extremely
small pieces which were painstakingly put
together.

Below
A modern grass hut from the Cameroons.
This is the type of hut suggested by the
pattern and size of stones found at Olduvai.
Easy to make and quite suitable for warm
climates, these huts are erected by many
nomadic hunters, sometimes put up each
night when on the move. Occasionally,
when suitable wood for the frame is scarce
the supports are carried from one site to
another.

Above

A lion kill in E. Africa such as this must have been the source of much of early Man's meat. Whether he was courageous enough to drive off the lions is not known, but he could have held his own against the hyaenas if he had several companions armed with sticks and stones. There is some evidence that Australopithecines sometimes fell victim to leopards, as what appear to be leopard teeth marks have been found on some skulls from S. Africa.

Overleaf

A group of Australopithecines who have made off with an antelope killed by lions which they are proceeding to cut up. The younger members of the party are keeping off the hyenas and vultures. It is probable that the Australopithecines obtained most of their bigger game by scavenging rather than by hunting. It seems unlikely that the small Australopithecines would have challenged the lions while they were still feeding but they were perfectly capable of keeping the smaller predators at bay long enough to get the greater part of the meat.

True Man

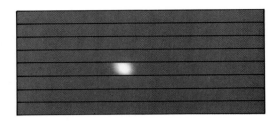

On reaching the second chapter in the story of Man's development we are on slightly more secure ground. It is not that there are fewer problems, but rather that the connection with the ape line has been severed forever and there is no doubt that we are now dealing with creatures whose human status is beyond dispute. This was not always the case.

As in the case of the Australopithecines it is easier to begin this part of the story in the order in which the various individuals were found.

During the controversy surrounding the publication of Darwin's *The Origin of Species,* and for a considerable time after, there was nothing which those in the scientific world who were prepared to support the idea of human evolution could accept as representing a definite stage in Man's ancestry.

The Gibraltar skull had been found in 1848 and the skull cap from the Neanderthal valley near Dusseldorf in 1856. The first disappeared into the local library to gather dust for nearly 50 years and the second was considered for some time as being a recent pathological specimen.

In 1891 Eugene Dubois, a Dutch army doctor stationed in Java, found, during excavations on the Solo river, a skull cap which was to have a profound effect on prehistoric human studies. The site at Trinil contained not only the skull cap but also a complete human femur and a considerable amount of animal bones. On the basis of the fauna the site was dated to the beginning of the Middle Pleistocene, about 500 000 years old. The skull showed several primitive traits; the walls are thick and there are heavy brow ridges, and, compared with the skull of modern Man, the vault is low. The brain capacity was estimated as being between 750cc–850cc, higher than any of the Australopithecines, but possibly within the range of the bigger East African skulls such as 1470. For a long time there was controversy over the status of the thigh bone. It was clearly human in form and showed that its owner stood upright like any modern man. Some anatomists considered that this bone did not belong to the skull which was found with it. On the assumption that the two bones did in fact belong (and fluorine tests confirm this) the new find was called *Pithecanthropus erectus,* the ape-man who walked upright.

For some years Java Man was, with the exception of Piltdown, the only representative of Man's ancestors between the later Neanderthals and the apes, a position which he seemed to fit into very well as he appeared in structural terms to lie about halfway along the line.

In 1908 a complete lower jaw was found during the digging of a sand pit at Mauer, near Heidelberg. The Heidelberg jaw was, by modern standards, very massive, with huge teeth and was clearly more primitive than the jaws known from any of the Neanderthals. The date for the Mauer sands, based on the fauna, was early Middle Pleistocene, between the first and second European glaciations, a chronological position similar to that of the Java material, and it is generally considered that Heidelberg and Java belong to the same stage of human development.

Since the original Java skull find, more material has emerged from the same area over the years and to this have been added the very extensive finds from China. Not far from Peking is the famous site of Choukoutien. For many years it was the source of 'dragon

bones' which, when ground up, provided efficacious tonics for the local drug stores. The finding of human teeth led to international interest which resulted in systematic excavations, research which the Chinese are continuing.

For some years the existence of *Sinanthropus pekinensis,* as these hominids were called, were based on no more than a single tooth found in 1927 and described by Davidson Black. The finding of parts of skulls continued for many years so that there are now at least fourteen skulls and eleven jaws, enough to give a very clear idea of these early inhabitants of China.

A further point of importance is that Choukoutien is a cave and was clearly an occupation site. Thus the material is not scattered as it was in the Java deposits.

Two interesting facts emerged from the excavation of this camp site: one that, judging from the animal bones, Peking Man was an efficient hunter; and secondly, for the first time there was clear evidence of the use of fire.

Also scattered among the food debris were stone implements made of quartzite and greenstone. These tools were not very complex, consisting only of choppers and large flakes, but nevertheless they would have filled all the requirements for processing the carcasses of the game hunted at that time.

The original Peking skull, probably that of a woman, appears to be a little more advanced than that from Java, the vault is higher and more rounded with an increased brain capacity; the range of the skulls is 915cc–1285cc, the last being within the range of modern Man.

The original Java specimens came from a deposit known as the Trinil Beds, which rest on an older series, the Djetis Beds, which have a more archaic fauna. These older Djetis Beds have also produced human material which in general form resembles that from the later Trinil Beds, though the skull of a child from Modjokerto seems to be less primitive than some of the others. It is necessary, however, to bear in mind that with all juvenile and infant skulls (this one being only two years old) the features of the adult are not yet developed, and the later very pronounced features are often missing.

Recent excavations at Lantian in the Shensi province of China have produced parts of a skull and jaw which belong to the same age as the population from the Djetis Beds of Java.

The two names, *Pithecanthropus* and *Sinanthropus,* given to the Java and Peking skulls respectively, suggest that they were sufficiently different to warrant their being placed in two separate genera. The modern view is that, far from being generically different, they are close enough to be put in one genus and furthermore are now included in the genus *Homo,* differentiated only on sub-specific level. This group, *Homo erectus,* once thought to have been confined to Asia, has recently been found in Africa with extensions into Europe.

In 1954 Arambourg, the French palaeontologist, found three jaws in an archaeological site at Ternifine in Algeria. One, Ternifine III, is almost complete and between them the majority of the teeth are present. The massiveness of these jaws made an obvious comparison with those from the Asian *Homo erectus,* and the similarities are considered so striking that they leave little doubt that these African peoples belong to the same group as the Asian *Homo erectus.*

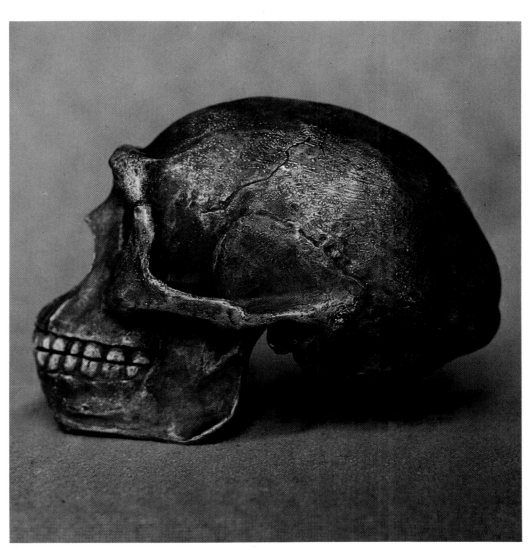

A reconstruction of the Peking skull from the deposits at Choukoutien in China – the so-called Peking skull.

None of the other skulls from this site were anything like as complete as the so-called Peking skull. The heavy brow-ridges are clearly recognized, as is the rather low vault. The brain size of around 900cc is well above that of the Australopithecines, though not much more than that calculated for 1470 from Lake Rudolf. The teeth are still large and the lower part of the face is thrust well forward.

Primitive as this skull may appear, owners of this type were efficient hunters and users of fire and makers of stone tools.

Many of the fossil bones found by chance ended up in Chinese drug stores where, under the name 'dragon's bones', they were ground up and used as medicine. Von Koenigswald found 47 teeth of a very large hominid in a number of drug stores in Hong Kong and China, and eventually more in cave deposits in south China. There is some doubt as to where these teeth should be placed since they are very large. It has been suggested that they might represent a form of *Australopithecus*.

Found associated with the human material were several hundred stone tools, and a rich mammalian fauna, indicating that this was a living site. The animals represented were elephant, zebra, rhinoceros, camel and several forms of antelope, giant wart-hog, giant baboon and, of particular interest, sabre-tooth cats.

There is so far no radiometric dating for this site, but the fauna suggests an early Middle Pleistocene date, a date comparable with the upper part of Bed II at Olduvai, which may begin as early as one million years ago.

It is again necessary to turn to Olduvai to continue the story following the disappearance of the last of the Australopithecines. In the upper part of Bed II the main industry represented is a developed form of the pebble chopper complex originally seen in the lower part of Bed I, dating to about 1·7 million. The developed Olduwan tools of upper Bed II are dated to about one million years—a very slow progress. We are no more certain as to who made this developed Olduwan than we are with the earlier Olduwan, certainly Zinj continues into the upper part of Bed II, though this does not necessarily imply that the industry is his. At the very top of Bed II came the greater part of a skull cap which is clearly more developed than any of the Australopithecines. Homo 9, as he is called, has an estimated brain capacity of 1 000cc and this, as well as the general form of the skull, clearly relate it to Homo erectus from the Far East.

Both the jaws from Ternifine and this skull from Olduvai clearly show that representatives of Homo erectus were as active in Africa as they were in Asia and at approximately the same time.

Before leaving Africa and following Homo erectus elsewhere there are two more areas which we need to consider. The first takes us back to the site of Swartkrans. In addition to Australopithecus robustus there was the suggestion that there might be another hominid present. The main components of this individual are a few jaw fragments and they are clearly more developed than those from Australopithecus. In addition to the physical differences there also appears to be a difference in time. Some anatomists originally considered that this later material was within the range of the other Australopithecines, but the general consensus of opinion is that it represents a variety of Homo erectus.

The most recent find of Homo erectus in Africa comes, like so much of the early material, from the vicinity of Lake Rudolf. In 1976 Richard Leakey found an almost complete skull which was clearly a member of the erectus group. The value of this find lies not only in the good state of the specimen but in the fact that it has a radiometric date of somewhere between one and 1·5 million years.

The last area to consider is Europe, which brings us back to the Heidelberg jaw. The similarity between the Heidelberg jaw and those from the Asian sites has already been mentioned and there is little doubt that the owner of the jaw belongs to the same stage of human development as those from Java, China and Africa.

For a long time the Heidelberg jaw was the only evidence of the presence of Homo erectus in Europe but recently other possible contenders have come to light. One such came from the site of Vertesszöllös, not far from Budapest. Like so much of the more recent human material to emerge, there is very little available, in this case only four milk teeth and part of the back of a skull, the occipital bone. Although originally classed as Homo erectus there is some doubt as to the exact standing of the Hungarian skull, since the outline of the skull bone seems to be nearer to modern Man than to Homo erectus. One is tempted to see this skull as being a more advanced specimen along the road towards the next stage of human development rather than a typical member of Homo erectus. The date given to the Hungarian skull is between the two peaks of the second, or Mindel glacial–about 500 000 years or roughly the same as the Peking skulls.

So far we have concentrated on the physical development and said little about the tools associated with the various members of Homo erectus. While it seems clear that the tools found with the members of the Australopithecines are fairly uniform over a considerable time span (some 2 million years), simple pebble choppers and flakes with little retouch, the tool kit of the next stage is not only more sophisticated, but varies according to the geographical distribution.

During the excavation of the site at Ternifine in Algeria several hundred implements were found. Unlike the earlier choppers these were well made hand-axes, a tool which was to continue in use until the beginning of the Last Glaciation. Named after two sites in northern France, Abbeville and St Acheul, a suburb of Amiens, they are found from Cape Town to central England and as far east as India, though rare in Eastern Europe. The majority are core tools, but some of the later examples are made of large flakes. These hand-axes seem to have served as a general purpose implement over a wide variety of environments.

The earliest form, the Abbevillian hand-axe, is rather crude and made only with a stone hammer which gives it a rough appearance. The later, Acheulian examples, are much better made, blocked out with a stone hammer, and completed with hard wood or bone implements, making it possible to obtain a fine finish, which in the later stages produced very beautiful tools. In addition to the hand-axes the Acheulian also contained flake tools, many derived from the hand-axe waste flakes; these were used for cutting and, particularly in the north, for scraping, possibly for skins.

In addition to Ternifine, hand-axes have also been found at Olduvai. The earliest came from the same horizon as the Homo erectus skull, Homo 9, but there was no direct association between the human remains and the implements, though there is a reasonable assumption that Homo 9 was responsible for them and was thus contemporary with the tool-makers of the developed Olduwan.

It has not been possible to say exactly how these hand-axes originated, but several sites in North Africa show a succession from the pebble choppers of Olduwan type into simple hand-axes, and it is reasonable to assume that they represent the logical development from the earlier pebble tools. It is further assumed that Africa was the original home of the hand-axe and that it spread north and east sometime during the early part of the Middle Pleistocene. We have however seen that not all of the Homo erectus groups were hand-axe makers, and that the industry associated with Peking Man is one of large flakes and simple chopping tools not dissimilar from those found in the later stages of the Olduwan.

Neither were the inhabitants of Vertesszöllös makers of hand-axes, instead their tool kit consisted of very small choppers and flakes, some of the choppers being so small that they would have been rather difficult to use if they were intended for cutting up game.

The available evidence shows that during the early part of the Middle Pleistocene, from about 1 million years to about 500 000 years (the time range of the known Homo erectus groups, in Asia, Africa and Europe) there appear to have been two different tool-making traditions, one based on hand-axes, centred on Africa, and the other on flakes and chopping tools, represented by the groups from Asia. Where the pebble industries from Europe originated is uncertain, but there is increasing evidence for pebble tool complexes in Europe, very similar to the Olduwan, though these are not as early, as far as we know, as those from East Africa.

To what extent can we reconstruct the life-styles of these early hominids? Judging from the available dates, they cover a period from one million years or more to about 500 000 years, a much shorter time than the Australopithecines. During this time range they show some development, at any rate in Asia where Peking Man is clearly more advanced than early Java and Lantian, and there is also some difference between the skulls from the two Java beds. It is too early to say to which group the Lake Rudolf or the other African examples belong.

That Homo erectus was a tool-maker is clear from all the regions though there is a difference between those of Asia and Africa, Europe being closer to Asia. Why there is this difference is not yet understood and will not be until we have a great deal more material.

The human remains that have emerged, though tantalizingly inadequate, allow us to make an intelligent guess as to their physical appearance, at least as far as the skeleton is concerned. We know that they walked fully upright as the leg bone from Java is almost identical to modern Man. A further suggestion is that its owner was not so much tall as robust, with well co-ordinated limbs and probably efficient hands, since he was a tool-maker and obviously a competent hunter. Moreover, in the later stages he seems to have mastered the use of fire, though we do not, of course, know if he was capable of lighting it.

There has been a great deal of argument as to what standards of

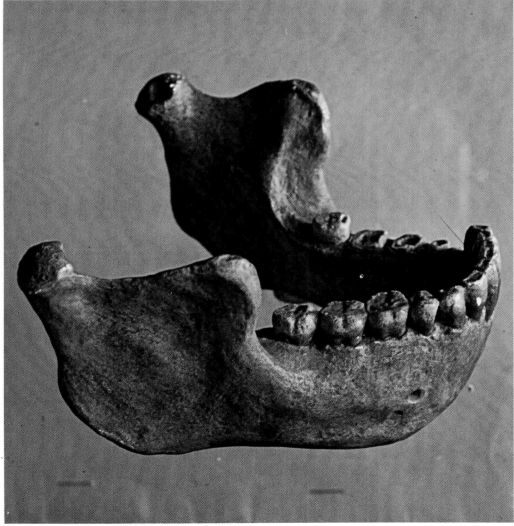

Left
The *Homo erectus* skull from Olduvai, *Homo* 9. This specimen came from the upper part of Bed II, and is the first occurrence of this type at Olduvai. Although no tools were found in the site from which it came, there are hand-axes at this level in other parts of the gorge, and it is assumed that these were made by *Homo* 9, or Chellian Man as this creature was called. The dating of this part of Bed II is not very certain, but in view of the recent discovery of a similar skull from deposits at Lake Rudolf, which are estimated to be over a million years old, this is probably the right order of magnitude for *Homo* 9, since it would put him in the same time-range as the Java skulls from the early Djetis Beds.

Below left
This massive lower jaw was found in the Mauer Sands near Heidelberg. The associated fauna suggests early Middle Pleistocene, just before the second or Mindel Glaciation. No tools were found in the deposit and no other fragments of the skull exist, so it is difficult to say in which category this jaw should be placed. It appears to be roughly the same age as *Homo erectus* from China, and it bears some resemblance to it, but some anatomists are reluctant to class it with the rest of the *Homo erectus* material until more material is found.

Overleaf
This is a view of the Lower Loam and Lower Gravel at Swanscombe, England. The gravel at the bottom is from a fairly fast-flowing river, and contains Clactonian tools washed in from the banks, but very little animal bone. Above is the Lower Loam, which contains fine sediments, laid down under marshy conditions with land surfaces forming from time to time. On these land surfaces Clactonian Man was making his stone tools and cutting up the game that he hunted on the banks of the river not far away.

communication *Homo erectus* had achieved, to what extent could he speak and are we justified in talking about the possibility of language? Whatever his range of language he was certainly capable of transmitting information, since by this time many basic ideas would have been transmitted from one generation to another; further, if there was communal hunting, as the evidence suggests, then *Homo erectus* would need to communicate plans and supervise the operation.

If tool-making and the transmission of ideas implies some speech then we must accredit a form of language to the earlier Australopithecines and their contempories, though this was probably at a much lower level than that of *Homo erectus.*

What of *Homo erectus*'s origins? In Africa 1470, or something very like him, would seem to be a reasonable candidate for the position of *Homo erectus*'s immediate ancestor, implying that the three species of *Australopithecus* were not on the main human line. So far nothing quite comparable to 1470 has yet come from the Far East though it has been suggested that the large teeth found in drug stores in Hong Kong and China and later jaw fragments from a cave in China may have belonged to an Asian version of *Australopithecus.*

This creature, named *Giganthropus,* has teeth much larger than those of *Homo erectus* and could be either an *Australopithecus* or belong to some side branch come to a dead end. Unfortunately, there is no clear date for the Chinese cave material but it was associated with a fauna which may be Middle Pleistocene. However, if this creature was ancestral to *Homo erectus* he must have appeared at a far earlier date.

When the original *Homo erectus* material was found in the Trinil beds in Java, a date somewhere in the early part of the Middle Pleistocene–roughly comparable with the second or Mindel Glaciation in Europe–was suggested. In European terms this would have implied a date of about 500 000 years for the Trinil skulls, with those from Peking somewhat later and those from the Djetis beds below the Trinil series earlier. Since these estimates were made potassium/argon dates have become available giving 0·5 million years for the top of the bed and 0·7 for the bottom. It would appear, then, that the Djetis beds and their contained skulls are probably as old as the upper part of Bed II at Olduvai with *Homo* 9, and probably not much younger than the *Homo erectus* skull from Lake Rudolf, which was discovered in 1976.

Before closing this chapter some mention must be made of Piltdown Man. This great hoax is of value because its acceptance gives some idea of scientific thinking at the time of its discovery and its exposure by the use of modern techniques ensures that it could not happen again.

The site at Piltdown in Sussex was a rather insignificant patch of gravel on the side of a road, and had no clear geological data. Charles Dawson, who came across the fossil, found the site while trying to trace some unusual gravel used for road-making. From his excavations he claimed to have found parts of a human jaw, and remains of elephant, hippopotamus and beaver.

By 1912, the date of the Piltdown discovery, the material from Java was already fully integrated into the general pattern of hominid knowledge as were, of course, the Neanderthals, but this was different. Here was clearly the missing link that everyone had been searching for: part-human and part-ape, for the jaw clearly resembled the latter. Since no one at the time had any reason to consider fraud, the majority of anatomists of the day spent a great deal of time trying to adapt the skull fragments to fit the jaw, producing a rather strange-looking creature as a result.

As more hominid material became available Piltdown Man seemed more and more unlikely until it became clear that he had no real place in human evolution. He was either a practical joke or, worse, a fake. The development of the fluorine technique finally consigned him to the latter category.

Fluorine comparison is based on the principle that bones of the same age from the same deposits will have the same amounts of fluorine, but tests made of the Piltdown material showed very different amounts in the various bones, that the skull and jaw could not be anything but modern, and that the whole assemblage was drawn from a variety of sources, the elephants for example from north Africa. Whoever perpetrated the fraud will probably never be known with certainty, but one result of the hoax was to subject new material to more stringent testing.

This shows a rhinoceros skull during the course of excavation at Swanscombe; the skull is base uppermost.

This horizon, the junction of the Lower Loam and the Lower Gravel, produced a great deal of animal bones, and may indeed have been a prehistoric rubbish pit. Associated with the bones were simple stone tools belonging to the Clactonian, which dates from about 250 000 years. With the rhinoceros were elephant, bear, fallow deer, ox and horse remains, indications of a temperate climate. In the gravels above and separated by a long interval was the Swanscombe skull associated with well made hand-axes. This skull dates from the Interglacial between the second and third Glaciations.

Below right
This is one of the attempts made to reconstruct the Piltdown skull fragments to fit the jaw. Provided there are enough pieces almost any shape of skull can be obtained. The anatomists of the day were, in addition, working on the false premise that the skull and jaw belonged to the same individual.

This reconstruction of the Piltdown pieces is interesting as an example of the discovery of precisely what these people had been looking for. If the Piltdown remains were older than the recently found skulls from Java, as the animals found with them suggested, then the skull must obviously look older, and this is what the reconstruction set out to achieve, producing something rather like the Australopithecines which were found much later.

The development of the fluorine tests for bone and its application to the Piltdown material led to a thorough investigation of the whole of the material, and it soon became clear that the whole thing was a hoax. The jaw was that of a modern ape, the wear on the teeth was produced by a file and the colour of the skull was the result of artificial staining.

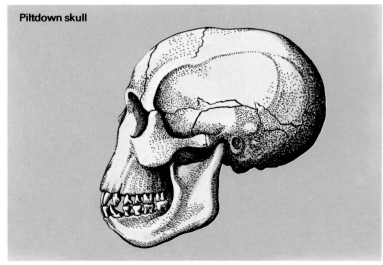

Piltdown skull

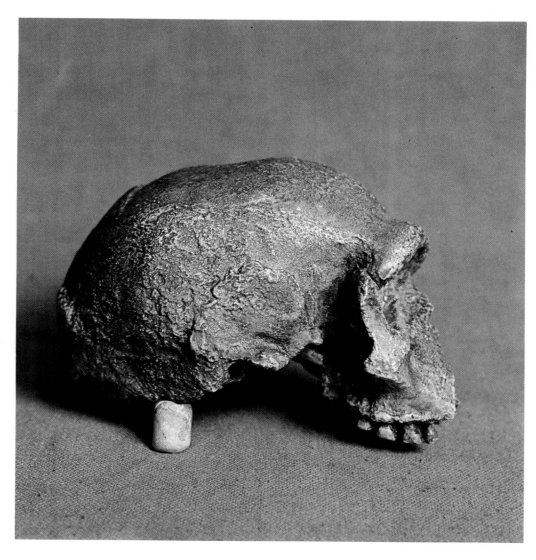

Left
This skull from Germany, unlike that from Swanscombe, is nearly complete though crushed on one side. Its age is roughly the same as that of the Swanscombe skull, and it was found with a very similar fauna, but no tools. The general shape of this Steinheim skull is sufficiently like that from Swanscombe to suggest that they are probably closely related, and that both had very similar faces. Both Steinheim and Swanscombe were originally considered to be the immediate ancestors of modern Man with the Neanderthals being a side branch, but it seems more likely that these two hominids gave rise to both Neanderthal and modern Man.

Below
Hand-axes made of flint from the same horizon as the Swanscombe skull.
These hand axes are found throughout Africa, western Europe and the Middle East and through to India. They seem to have served as general purpose tools and were probably used principally for butchering the larger animals. Many of them were found at the elephant butchering sites in Spain and they are frequent on similar sites in Africa. As a tool they die out in Europe at the beginning of the Last Glaciation, around 70 000 years ago.

Overleaf
This scene shows *Homo erectus* skinning a deer at the entrance to his cave. We know from China that this group were efficient hunters, although no tools suitable for spears have been found hence the fire-hardened wooden spear. By this time fire was in use and probably skins were also made use of; the mother and child are bringing up water from the valley.

Neanderthal Man

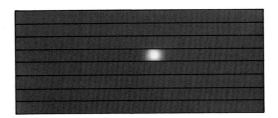

The Neanderthals, to give them their popular name, are the best known of Man's ancestors. This is partly because they were the first of the pre-*Homo sapiens* to be accorded recognition, but also because they are represented by more individuals than any other fossil hominid group.

The original find from the Neanderthal valley, near Dusseldorf, came from a limestone quarry and most probably from a cave in the cliff, though no animal remains nor archaeological material was found with it, or at least not recognized as such at the time. The date of its discovery, 1856, preceded Darwin's *The Origin of Species* by three years, and would seem to have provided the first evidence for a form primitive in appearance compared with ourselves and apparently well-equiped to fill the position of one of Man's forefathers.

Establishing the find from Neanderthal as being in the human lineage was far from plain sailing: firstly, it was not associated with anything which could give any clue as to its age, and, secondly, there was nothing more to work on than the skull cap with the very heavy brow ridges and the eye sockets. Lastly, no one had any clear idea what Man's ancestor would have looked like, even if such a thing was accepted which, even among the well informed, it was not.

Such scanty material would not have deterred the later anatomists used to dealing with the very incomplete specimens from China and Java, but to the early protagonists of human evolution the Neanderthal skull cap was not a very strong weapon and, not surprisingly, it aroused great controversy. Much of this heat would have been neutralized if the almost complete skull from Forbe's quarry in Gibraltar, found in 1848, had been properly described at the time.

The reaction of the anti-evolutionists was that either the skull was pathological or belonged to an idiot, which amounted to much the same thing. Such arguments for and against could have continued forever, but more finds over the next 50 years fully confirmed Neanderthal Man as a type and further supplied supporting evidence for his approximate place in time.

One of the early supporting specimens for the Neanderthal Man skull cap was found in a pit at La Naulette in Belgium in 1865. This find, a lower jaw, came from an organized excavation and was associated with bones of mammoth, woolly rhinoceros and reindeer. The main feature of this jaw was that it was without a chin and was clearly more primitive compared with the jaws of modern Man.

The idea that Neanderthal Man was no more than a pathological misfit was finally destroyed by the discovery of three human skeletons from a cave at Spy in the province of Namur, also in Belgium. The Spy cave was carefully excavated and the human remains were shown to be clearly associated with a fauna similar to that from Naulette and in addition there were stone tools which belonged to the owners of the skeletons. The reconstruction of Spy I, which was almost complete, showed a skull form very close to that from Neanderthal and a jaw resembling that from La Naulette; clearly these specimens were consistent in form and, whatever their position in the human family, they represented a distinct race, different in many respects from modern Man. Between 1886 and 1908 more examples came to light, but 1908 was a distinct

landmark in the story of Neanderthal Man, both physically and culturally; for it was in this year that A and J Bouyssonie and L Bardon excavated a small cave in a hillside at La Chapelle aux Saints, in the département of Corrèze in south-west France.

The finding of the old man of La Chapelle (for old he was) was a landmark because here was the first certain example of a Neanderthal burial, though the bodies from Spy and possibly even the original Neanderthal skull may have come from a burial also.

The site of the old man's resting-place was unusual. The cave, like many in France, contained occupation material in the form of broken bones, the remains of meals and a number of stone tools; clearly the rubbish of a home. At this cave, however, the roof was so low as to make standing impossible. The body lay on its back in a shallow grave dug in the floor and the head resting against the edge of the pit. It was apparently wedged in place with stones, and with the legs folded. Above the head were long bones and the foot of an ox, part of a funeral feast according to the excavators. Scattered throughout the fill of the grave and in the deposit above were a mass of stone implements, unusual in that the proportion of finished tools to waste flakes was far higher than in any other occupation site belonging to Neanderthal Man.

A second burial was found in the following year at the site of Le Moustier, in the Dordogne district of France, not far from La Chapelle. The site is also unusual in that there are two caves one above the other on the bank of the Vézère river. Both caves were occupied by Neanderthal Man as well as later peoples, which is not surprising in view of the splendid position of the site with the river running outside the entrance. The burial, in the lower cave, was that of a youth about sixteen years old.

There has been some criticism of the excavation methods employed but nevertheless there seems to be little doubt that the boy was deliberately buried like the old man. The body was on its right side with the right forearm under the head as though asleep; under the head was a bed of flint chips and near the right hand a late form of hand-axe. Also found in the grave were bones both burnt and split open, implying a similar food offering to that from La Chapelle.

Not far from Le Moustier, at the rock shelter of La Ferrassie, was found what can only be described as a Neanderthal cemetery. As at Le Moustier the Neanderthals were the earliest occupants of the shelter, but again they were followed by later inhabitants. The burials which have survived consist of two adults and two children, though there may originally have been more.

These bodies were not buried in the strict sense like those from the other two sites but were lying on the surface and covered with earth; in the case of one, the head was protected by slabs of stone. It has been suggested that at least one of the bodies was not moved after death but covered where it lay.

In the département of Charente, north west of the Dordogne, is La Quina, the site of a partially collapsed rock shelter. In 1911 Dr Henri Martin found an almost complete skull, probably that of a woman, and later the skull of an eight year old child. In all La Quina produced fragments of some nineteen individuals.

The finds described above give a very clear idea of Neanderthal Man, at least in western Europe. We have old age, from La Chapelle; youth from Le Moustier, and childhood from La Quina

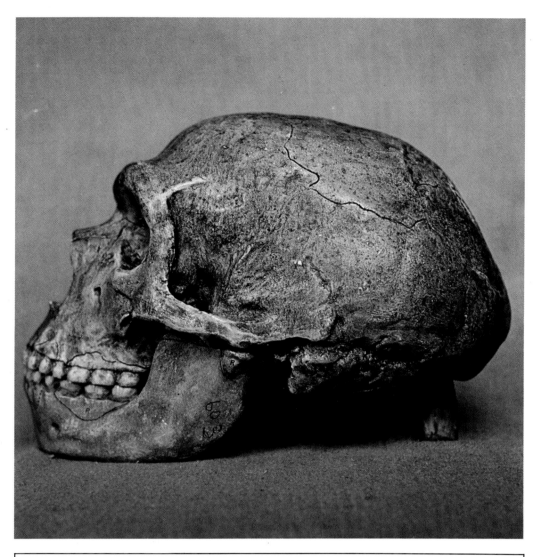

Left
This skull of the old man from the burial at La Chapelle aux Saints in south-west France is a very good example of the western or extreme type of Neanderthal Man as opposed to the less extreme variants from eastern Europe and the Middle East. He also has one of the largest brains recorded for Neanderthal Man, 1620cc. The age at death is uncertain, but he had already lost many of his teeth so he probably died somewhere around 45 years of age. Apart from its completeness, this is one of the earliest findings of a burial and the first to be properly described.

It has always been uncertain whether any grave goods were with the body as the fill of the cave was made up of occupation debris, thus making it impossible to say whether the tools and bones found with the body were put there at the time of the burial or were part of the filling of the grave. This burial was the first of many, not only in France but elsewhere, all showing the same respectful attitude towards the dead.

Below left
A drawing of the cave and burial at La Chapelle aux Saints at the time of the excavation. As can be seen, the cave roof is very low and it is almost impossible to stand upright in the cave itself, so it is doubtful whether it was used as a permanent home, though it would have served as a temporary shelter; particularly as the roof height increases towards the entrance. In the entrance were the remains of a hearth, and also a shallow trench said to have contained bones of bison. It has been suggested that this may have been the remains of a funeral feast. It is probable however that the earlier prehistorians were reading too much into the evidence and that this cave, which was apparently not often used because of its size, was pressed into service and all the bones and tools belonged to temporary occupations.

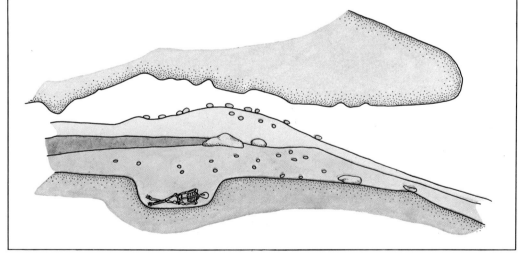

as well as both male and female adults. This material amply supported the claim that Neanderthal Man represented a clearly defined group of hominids not only different from modern Man but clearly much more developed than the hominids found in Java in 1890.

The early attempts to reconstruct Neanderthal Man met with only partial success in spite of the considerable amount of material available. This was partly because the early attempts were still influenced by what popular opinion considered Man's ancestor to have been, with the result that many of the early reconstructions show an individual not far removed from an ape. There are, however, sufficient remains to give us an overall picture, which is now probably much more accurate.

In spite of the rather low vault common to all the western Neanderthals, the brains of some of them are extremely large, that of La Chapelle being estimated at about 1600cc compared with the modern average of about 1500cc (Beethoven's skull is estimated at 1750cc). Not all of the Neanderthal brains reach the high figure of

La Chapelle and the average is about 1250cc.

In addition to the large head there are large jaws to accommodate the very big teeth—a characteristic of these jaws is the absence of a chin. One trait which is shared with many of the earlier hominids is the massive brow ridges, more developed in the males than the females. These brow ridges provide support for the muscles necessary to operate the large jaws and are a feature of feeding habits rather than part of an evolutionary process.

The limb bones are rather short and stout and the general height was probably not much over five feet (1·5 metres). The bones of both hands and feet are available and there is no doubt that Neanderthal Man not only walked fully upright but also had considerable manual dexterity. A rare find for so early an individual is a very well defined footprint from a site in Italy, showing a broad and rather flat foot, a flatness common among people who habitually go bare-footed.

As well as the tendency for the early anatomists to misconceive Neanderthal Man's overall appearance, there was a tendency to misrepresent his posture. Many of the early reconstructions were based on the most complete skeleton then available, La Chapelle, and show a short, stooping individual with head thrust well forward. Recent studies have shown that the posture suggested for La Chapelle was really due to acute osteoarthritis (not very surprising in a man over 45) and that he would have walked in his younger days much as modern Man.

Research over the last 70 years has not only thrown a great deal of additional light on Neanderthal Man and his distribution but also given us increasing information about his cultural development and way of life. The very large number of Neanderthals which have survived is due not only to the practice of burial but more to the fact that many of them, particularly in Europe, were living in caves which preserved both their skeletons and much of their tools in their original positions.

At the turn of the century the content of several European caves, mostly in France, were excavated much more systematically than before and it was apparent that the caves had been inhabited over a long period of time and that the successive groups of inhabitants belonged to several cultural types. In the majority of caves the Neanderthals were the original inhabitants and their stone industry, called Mousterian after Le Moustier, differed markedly from those that followed.

When the Mousterian was first recognized as a cultural complex it was described as essentially a flake industry, not very rich in tool types, consisting of rather thick scrapers and points. More detailed work of the Mousterian tool kits from various deposits, particularly in south-west France, has shown that the term Mousterian describes not one but at least five varieties. These differ partly in the techniques emloyed for the production of the flakes and partly in the differences of the various tool types. Some varieties, like that associated with the Mousterian youth, had heart-shaped hand-axes and a very high percentage of scrapers. With another technique, over 80 per cent of its tool flakes have irregular notches on the edges, the purpose of which is not known.

In terms of technique one method of flake production is very complicated and requires not only a great deal of planning but also considerable skill. The method consists of shaping the core in such a way that a flake of predetermined shape and size can be detached. This preparation is for one flake only and if further flakes of similar shape are required the core must be re-prepared. Other Mousterian groups used manufacturing techniques which gave less control over the size and shape of the flakes and resulted in tools which were generally thick and more irregular; further, if a particular shape was needed then it could only be obtained by extensive retouching. The various groups made use of both methods.

The Neanderthals occupied western Europe during the first two stages of the Last or Würm Glaciation with a probable date-range from about 70 000 to 35 000 years ago, the later dates being based on a number of Carbon 14 determinations. Although this represents their main position in the sequence there is evidence of earlier habitation by the group in the previous Interglacial. During the first two phases of Würm, Europe was generally very cold with not much improvement during the short interstadial.

The Neanderthals are usually associated with the mammoth, woolly rhinoceros and reindeer, and, judging from the animals they killed, the Neanderthals must have been efficient hunters capable of bringing down a wide variety of game. Furthermore, during the appropriate seasons they were also gatherers. They also used fire extensively, since it was essential to their survival and, when considering the number of tools suitable for preparing skins, it is apparent that they were probably fully clothed in the skins of the animals they hunted. There is also some evidence that they improved their caves by erecting some form of shelter in the entrance, made either of skins or brushwood.

Though the best-known sites in western Europe are either caves or rock shelters there are many open sites, particularly in the vicinity of rivers such as the Somme and Seine in France and the lower reaches of the Thames. There is no clear evidence as to whether these were used as summer camps or if the inhabitants had any form of shelter.

So far we have only discussed Neanderthal Man and his Mousterian culture in western Europe, the so-called 'classic' area, but men of this type with very similar tools occur over wide areas of the Old World. Variants of either Neanderthal Man or his tools

have been found all over Europe, as well as in Africa, north of the Sahara, and across the Middle East. Within this wide range the tools and methods of manufacture are very similar in spite of considerable differences in climate.

In the Levant, particularly Israel, Lebanon and Iraq, quite typical Mousterian tools have been found in both caves and open sites. At Mount Carmel, near Haifa, two caves almost adjoining have produced individuals of different types: one, from Tabun, was very similar to the 'classic' type of Europe, but the others, from Skhul, appear to be slightly more advanced with high vaults to their skulls. Although the Skhul people still have rather pronounced brow ridges, they resemble modern Man very closely. From Shanidar in north Iraq came a number of Neanderthals very like those from Tabun. How close these two types are in time is not very clear, but the tools associated with them are almost identical.

Two unusual pieces of information have emerged from these Middle East sites. One of the bodies from Mount Carmel was found to have a wound in the hip. This had formed a hole from

Below
This view of the Vézère River, a tributary
of the Dordogne River in south-west
France, was taken from a small cave high up
in the cliff, and it is the kind of view
prehistoric Man must have had from many
of the caves in the area. While involving a
long walk down to the river, the altitude
nevertheless gave a measure of protection to
the occupants and, for hunters of herd
animals, a very good view of the
surrounding country. Many of these French
caves were occupied by a succession of people
and some were in use for 30 000 years.

Overleaf
Neanderthal Man killing a woolly rhinoceros.
It is uncertain whether the larger animals
like these and the mammoths were attacked
direct and there is evidence of their being
bogged, but digging pits is a perfectly
logical alternative and is a practice used
occasionally by modern hunters. Certainly
this method would be far safer than facing
what must have been an extremely
dangerous animal. Stone tools similar to the
spear points are frequently found in
Mousterian deposits.

A rather fanciful 19th century picture of a
cave man attacking a cave bear.

These bears, which survived in Europe
until the end of the Last Glaciation, were
considerably larger than the modern Kodiak
bears, the largest of the modern land bears.
Their bones are found in a number of cave
sites and they are also depicted in various
wall paintings. In certain areas the
Mousterians seemed to have collected the
skulls, and it has been suggested that this
was some form of bear cult not unlike that
of the modern Ainu from Japan. Such
abstract ideas will of course never be proved.

It is not known for certain whether these
bears hibernated but it is very likely that
they did and it may have been during their
winter sleep that they were killed by the
Mousterian hunters.

Opposite top

A group of four Mousterian flint tools.
Some, like the second from the left, were
made by a prepared core technique, and this
example, which would have been very
suitable for a spear point, came off the core
in this shape because the core was prepared
in advance. This careful preparation meant
that many usable flakes were produced
which required little or no further working.
The other three are long flakes with very
sharp edges and would have been used as
knives.

The Mousterian tool-kit also contained a
wide variety of scraping tools, presumably
for preparing skins, and some Mousterian
groups also used small hand-axes. Although
the majority of Mousterian tools are made
of rather short flakes, there are several
varieties of Mousterian recognized, some
with special scrapers, some with hand-axes,
and others suggestive of groups of a very
meagre tool-kit. Various explanations for
this variety have been suggested: tribal
traditions, tools made at different times of
the year, and tools reflecting responses to
different environments. It is possible that the
explanation is a combination of all three.

which it was possible to make a clear cast. The weapon used was a
sharpened stake and the victim seems to have been bending down
when attacked. The signs of some healing of the bone imply that he
lived for a little time after but may have died subsequently of blood
poisoning. The other unusual occurrence was from the cave at
Shanidar. One of the adult burials was found to have a very high
pollen level in the grave fill, suggesting that he had been laid on a
pillow of wild flowers.

Returning to the point where we stopped in the last
chapter—Peking Man—we are faced with a marked time gap which
must be filled, but in addition there is a big evolutionary jump
from Peking Man to the Neanderthals of western Europe. Even
allowing for a late date of about 500 000 years for the more
developed forms of *Homo erectus,* there is still more than 400 000
years for which we cannot account.

Accepting for the moment that Peking Man and Vertesszöllös
represent the same general stage of development, we also find that
they occurred at approximately the same time, the middle of the
second or Mindel Glaciation. This means that the following
Interglacial, the third Glacial, the Riss and the Interglacial
immediately preceding the Last Glaciation, as far as hominids are
concerned, remain unaccounted for.

To make some headway with this problem, it is better to start
with an investigation of Europe since our information for this
region is more complete than anywhere else.

For the greater part of the period between the Mindel Glaciation
and the early part of the Würm, western Europe was occupied by
hand-axe makers who probably came from Africa where this tool
appears to have originated. When this movement took place is not
very clear, but makers of crude hand-axes of Abbevillian type were
living on the banks of the Somme sometime during the Mindel
Glaciation. These hand-axe makers do not appear to have been the
only occupants of western Europe during this time nor indeed the
earliest. We have already seen that at Vertesszöllös in Hungary
hominids, apparently of *Homo erectus* type, were making pebble
tools and, from a recently discovered cave at Vallonet on the
French Riviera, came similar tools which may date from the end of
the Lower Pleistocene.

Whatever their priority may have been in terms of occupation,
from the Mindel Glaciation to the beginning of Würm the
Acheulian hand-axe makers dominated western Europe. They lived
mainly in the river valleys and hunted a wide range of animals
including elephant and rhinoceros as well as smaller game. In
northern France and southern Britain, areas rich in flint-bearing
chalk, they produced some superb hand-axes as well as
making use of flake tools.

Who were these hand-axe makers? In spite of the thousands of
tools that have been found which undoubtedly belong to them and
the large number of sites uncovered, we know very little about
these people, either concerning their physical appearance or their

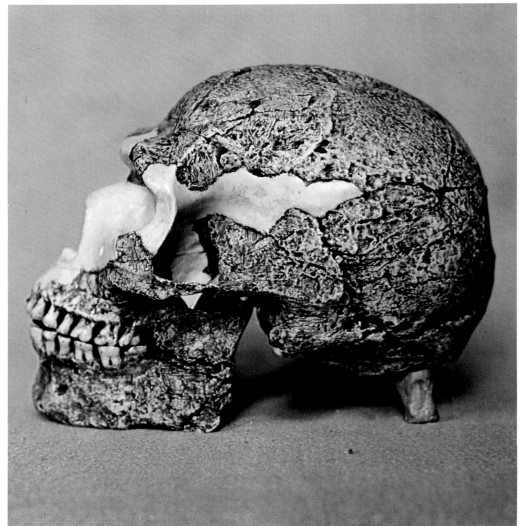

Left

The Skhul V skull from the cave of Skhul, Mount Carmel, is the best preserved out of a large number of bones representing at least 11 individuals. Skhul V and Skhul IV, both of which were almost complete skeletons, were clearly buried in the floor of the cave which contained occupation debris.

In many respects the skull is more like modern Man than the Neanderthals, the back of the head being very well filled out, though the heavy brow ridges are still present. The brain capacity, 1 500 cc, is in the upper range of the Neanderthals, and is above their average. Although these Skhul remains were clearly from burials there is not much evidence of grave goods, with the possible exception of a pig's jaw in the arms of Skhul V. One of the skeletons had a large hole in the hip made from a sharpened stick, a wound from which the man did not survive for very long.

way of life. The majority of their tools and the bones of the animals they hunted are mostly found washed into the gravels of the rivers by which they lived and, although much of this material has not been carried very far, their camp sites have been destroyed.

Two sites in central Spain, however, give some idea of at least one aspect of their lives. Both sites are elephant-butchering places; the animals apparently having been driven into soft ground and dismembered on the spot. In one case the long tusks seem to have been used as levers to turn the huge carcases over to get to the meat on the underside. Most of the Acheulian sites in Europe are open stations, but towards the end of the period caves were used though to a lesser extent than by the Neanderthals.

At only one site in Europe have human remains been found in direct association with early hand-axes. The site at Swanscombe, on the southern bank of the lower Thames, consists of thick deposits of sand and gravel derived from the river when flowing very much higher than at present. There are two distinct periods of gravel formation; the earlier, the Lower Gravel and Lower Loam, contains an industry of flakes and simple pebble choppers which might be in the tradition of Vertesszöllös and Vallonet. This assemblage of tools named Clactonian after Clacton-on-Sea in Essex, is not very well understood. The tool types are very simple with little more than roughly retouched flakes and pebble choppers. The Clactonian sites at Swanscombe and elsewhere are associated with the bones of elephant, rhinoceros and particularly a large form of fallow deer, all of which seem to have been hunted.

Studies of the various species of animal skulls and the pollen which has recently been extracted indicate a temperate climate, and these people seem to have been living in Britain some time during the early part of the Interglacial between Mindel and Riss, though their original occupation of Britain may have started earlier.

Above the Clactonian river gravels and separated from them by an unknown time interval are the Middle Gravels, from which have come a fauna, very similar to that from below, and thousands of well made hand-axes. Found in the same horizon as the hand-axes was what is known as the Swanscombe skull. This consists of three pieces, the back or occipital and the two sides, the parietal bones; the frontal bone and the face as well as the teeth are missing. The three pieces, found over a period of nearly 25 years fit perfectly and clearly belong to the same individual, possibly a woman. Following the Middle Gravels are deposits clearly laid down during cold conditions, suggesting the onset of the Riss Glaciation.

As a representative of Man between *Homo erectus* and the Neanderthals (as this skull's chronological position suggests) the appearance of this skull is rather surprising. At first sight the Swanscombe skull seems to be much more progressive than the classic Neanderthals, for she has a well-rounded skull comparable to modern Man, though the bones are much thicker. This is not what would have been expected for the forerunner of the extreme Neanderthals of France and Germany.

The nearest hominid in time and far more complete than Swanscombe is the skull from Steinheim in Germany found in 1933. Though no tools were found with the Steinheim skull the associated fauna of straight-tusked elephant and the temperate rhinoceros suggest the same Mindel/Riss Interglacial as at Swanscombe. The skull is almost complete though badly crushed on one side, yet, unlike Swanscombe, it has an almost whole face and some teeth. The back of the Steinheim skull resembles the general outline of Swanscombe, but the heavy brow ridges suggest a relationship with the later Neanderthals; whatever its exact position in the evolutionary picture it has very little resemblance to *Homo erectus*.

In addition to these two hominids several later fragments have come to light though none of these probably precede the Riss Glaciation. From the cave of Montmaurin in the Pyrenees came a well-preserved jaw. The date of this specimen is uncertain, but it may be as old as the material from Swanscombe and Steinheim, and it has even been suggested that it could have fitted the Steinheim skull.

Recently the well-preserved front of a skull from a cave also in the Pyrenees, has emerged which most likely dates from the Riss Glaciation and has a very Neanderthal appearance.

Few anatomists would claim that these early skulls were true Neanderthals, but there were certainly some of them around during the latter part of the Last Interglacial, associated with temperate

faunas. One such example comes from the cave at Krapina in what is now Yugoslavia. Found between 1899 and 1906 during the course of excavation, the remains, though very fragmentary, represent at least thirteen individuals: men, women and children. The fact that some of the human bones show signs of burning have led some prehistorians to believe that Neanderthal Man practised cannibalism, although it seems more likely that the bones became mixed with other bones in the hearths of later Neanderthal occupants. There is, however, some evidence of at least ritual cannibalism. From the cave of Monte Circeo in Italy a skull was found resting on the ground surrounded by a ring of stones. What is interesting is that the base of the skull had been broken open, possibly to extract the brain. In addition, at Saccopastore, also in Italy, came two typical Neanderthal skulls, and like Krapina associated with a temperate fauna–though Italy at this time was never as cold as the northern regions.

Outside Europe, examples of Neanderthal Man have been found along the north African coast and down to Ethiopia as well as in the Middle East. Over this range the accompanying archaeological materials is very similar to the Mousterian culture from Europe, in fact some of the Mousterian from Tunisia is strikingly like that from La Ferrassie.

In Africa, south of the Sahara, the place of the Mousterian culture is represented by local industries also based on flakes and similar to the northern industries developed from the later stages of the Acheulian culture. These African Middle Stone-Age industries, as they are called, are based on the same techniques for producing flakes as the European cultures but the overall tool assemblages differ.

Associated with one of these Middle Stone-Age industries is one of the best-preserved of all the fossil skulls, that of Rhodesian Man. Like so many such finds this skull was discovered during quarrying at Broken Hill in Zambia. The site was a limestone hill rich in lead and zinc. Although it was not recognized at the time, the fossil material was probably located originally in a cave, like the site at Neanderthal and that of the original Gibraltar skull. Found with the skull were leg and arm bones which, because of their modern appearance, were thought to have been intrusive. Extensive tests of all the human bones have shown that they have the same mineral content and are from the same horizon.

Rhodesian Man has given rise to some controversy. To some anatomists he represents an African version of Neanderthal Man, but to others he is much nearer to modern Man, in spite of the heavy brow ridges.

Further south in Cape Province came a skull cap of a similar individual, found with late forms of hand-axes which have been carbon-dated from another site at around 58 000 years. This is well within the range of the northern Neanderthals.

Moving eastwards from the Middle East where at least two representatives of the Neanderthals have been found, hominid discoveries comparable to Neanderthal Man are very scarce. At Teshil-Tash in Russian Uzbekistan was found the grave of an eight year old Neanderthal boy. The deposit in which he was found contained Mousterian tools, and the grave was covered with the horns of wild goats, possibly in the form of an offering.

In Java the latest of the three hominid layers, the Ngandong series, has produced skulls which compare with those of Europe and the Middle East. The Solo skulls named after the Solo river are claimed as being the eastern equivalent of the Neanderthals. Some see them as being closer to the *Homo erectus* found in the same area.

For a long time it seemed that human evolution took place in four distinct stages: *Australopithecus, Homo erectus,* Neanderthal and finally *Homo sapiens.* As more material became available this rather simplified picture began to break down. The discovery, first of *Homo habilis* and later 1470, cast considerable doubt as to the position of the Australopithecines. The appearance of intermediate forms between *Homo erectus* and the Neanderthals, some of which were more like modern Man than the Neanderthals they were supposed to have preceded, led to some re-thinking, certainly regarding the relationship between the Neanderthals and *Homo sapiens.*

One solution to this problem which has recently gained considerable support is that *Homo erectus* did not give rise to the Neanderthals which in turn produced *Homo sapiens,* but that both developed along their own lines as variants of a common ancestor

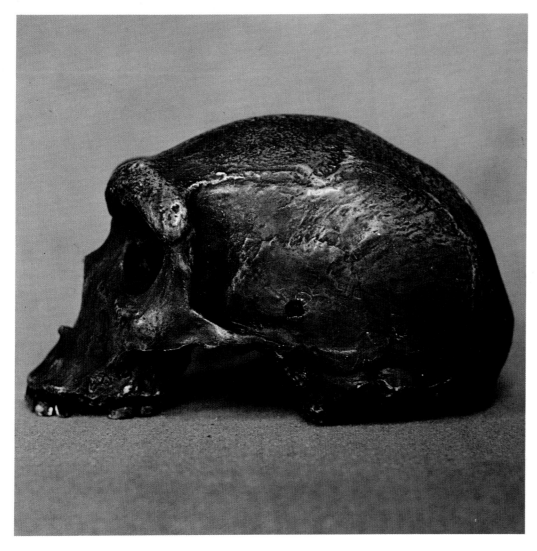

Left
Rhodesian Man is one of the best preserved of the early skulls. It was found in 1921 at Broken Hill, Zambia, during quarrying in small limestone hills containing lead and zinc ores. Whether or not the hill contained an occupied cave cannot now be ascertained, but along with the skull were found some long bones and a few stone tools. For some time there was doubt as to whether the skull and long bones belong to the same period. But tests show they are of the same age.

At one time Rhodesian Man was considered as belonging to the Neanderthals, who are well represented in North Africa. There are, however, some differences particularly in the limbs which are much more like modern Man's. It seems likely that by the end of the last Glaciation in Europe Man was already emphasizing regional differences, and the Rhodesian skull suggests a local variation of the more typical Neanderthals further north. The archaeological material found with the skull is what is called Middle Stone Age, and in some respects it is like the Mousterian.

Below
The Solo Man skulls, eleven in all, came from the latest of the Java fossil deposits, the Ngandong Beds, whose date is at least Upper Pleistocene. The population from Solo has presented some problems. They are clearly much more advanced than the local *Homo erectus* and the skull is well-rounded, but the brain size would put them within the lower limits of the Neanderthal range.

Some anatomists have categorized Solo Man as advanced *Homo erectus,* but the more recent view is that they are a local variant of the Neanderthals, and they have been named *Homo sapiens soloensis.*

Most of the Solo skulls show some signs of injury, but it is not clear how they met their deaths. A few stone tools have been found in the same deposit, but there are not enough to say what they represent.

Overleaf
Spending the winter in relative comfort, late Neanderthal Man was a skilful hunter and craftsman. The extremely cold winters would have made the wearing of skin clothing essential and there is some archaeological evidence of some simple structures erected in the interior of caves.

who has still to be identified and universally acknowledged.

If this idea is right then it means that *Homo sapiens,* the classic Neanderthals of Europe, and the less extreme forms from the Middle East, and probably Rhodesian Man, all belong to the same species, *Homo sapiens,* and only differ from each other on a sub-specific level. Some anatomists even class the Skhul skulls with modern Man. To separate these human variants they have been labelled, *Homo sapiens sapiens, Homo sapiens neanderthalensis, Homo rhodesiensis;* whether Solo Man is to be included with them is not yet clear, although some refer to *Homo sapiens soloensis.*

This wider grouping of Upper Pleistocene Man goes some way towards explaining the apparent sudden disappearance of Neanderthal Man in western Europe and his abrupt replacement by modern Man. If one assumes, first, that the marked traits of typical Neanderthal Man were acquired and not evolutionary, second, that they were not dominant factors and, third, with the removal of the circumstances which gave rise to them, they gradually receded, then there is no need to evoke the idea of species extinction.

It has been suggested that the Neanderthal brain, though in some cases as large as or even larger than the human average, was less complex and therefore in certain aspects inferior, particularly in intellectual capacity. This may have been partly true. Probably his range of speech was less than that of his successors and it is also possible that he had a lower level of abstract thought.

Unfortunately very little of his culture has come down to us and we are left only with his stone tools with which to make an assessment of his intellectual make-up. Had we had as much material available as we have from the later periods we may well have gained a better impression of our cousin.

That Neanderthal was a success there can be no doubt. He managed to survive in a wide variety of environments, some markedly hostile; his stone industry was complex and he showed great technical skill. In spite of his large brain it was less complex than that of modern Man. Yet the burial of his kin suggests some sensitivity. This was not the half-ape half-man of the early prehistorians, but an individual of great vigour who over the years gradually lost his identity.

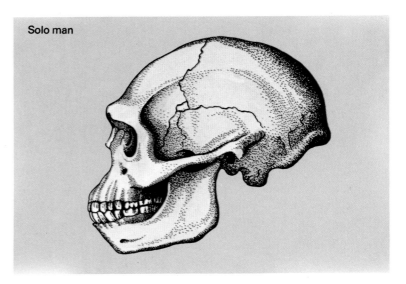

Solo man

Homo sapiens sapiens

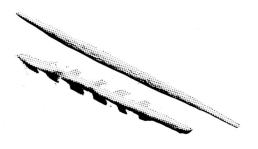

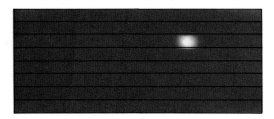

Homo sapiens, Man the Wise—is this the end of the road, or the beginning of another cycle leading to further development or perhaps extinction? Biological extinction seems unlikely as we are no longer so dependent on our environment. We can stockpile our food and, with air conditioning, cut across climatic zones. If we become extinct it will be of our own making.

Whatever Man's ultimate fate may be, we are only concerned here with modern Man while he still shared subsistence levels with his predecessors, *Homo erectus* and Neanderthal Man, both hunters and gatherers, and *Homo sapiens sapiens,* doing much the same thing until the adoption of farming.

Before trying to review the possible origins of *Homo sapiens sapiens,* it is necessary to consider to what extent he differs from his predecessors, what traits he has gained and lost, and what makes him apparently greatly superior to the hominids which have gone before.

The differences between Neanderthal Man (using the term in the broad sense) and his successor is not very great and, with the less specialized forms of Neanderthal Man, like those from Eastern Europe and the Middle East, the two hominids almost merge. It thus becomes extremely difficult to say into which group they should be placed. Apart from the skull, the differences between the two are slight, so it is with the skull rather than with the post-cranial parts that the comparisons must be made.

The brain size of Neanderthal Man over the whole range is about 300 cc less than ours, although in the case of the skull from La Chapelle, it reached a cubic capicity greater than the modern average. It has always been argued that brain size alone is not significant; what matters is the brain's complexity and of course the development of particular areas, the most important being the frontal lobes.

If the human lineage is followed back to *Homo erectus* and concentrated on the skull alone, we can see that, leaving aside the effect on the skull of large teeth and jaws, there are two related changes taking place. Firstly the actual brain capacity is increasing, which of course alters the actual size of the skull, and secondly there is a very marked change in its overall shape. The degree of backward slope of the forehead is not greatly different between the advanced *Homo erectus,* Steinheim Man and the extreme Neanderthals. The change which is taking place at this time is the filling out of the back of the head.

Comparing Neanderthal and modern Man, the changes in skull form are in the front, with the angle of the frontal bone rising until it becomes almost vertical. The change of this angle is due to the greater development of the frontal areas of the brain, which are those concerned largely with intelligence. This brain development can also be seen from the casts taken from inside the skulls. These show that the Neanderthal brain is much less developed and that the modern brains, though sometimes smaller, have a far bigger surface area due to extensive folding.

We have already seen that the grouping of several hominids—Neanderthal, Rhodesian Man and possibly Solo—under the same genus and species as modern Man accentuates the fine line which separates them. Nevertheless, what we now call *Homo sapiens sapiens* is clearly superior to the others, and this superiority will become more apparent when we come to consider his way of life.

During the first two stages of the Last Glaciation, down to about 35 000 years ago, Neanderthal Man held sway in western Europe. He lived in caves, where available, as well as in open camps. Since he lived much of this time during very severe climatic conditions, his powers of survival were obviously very high. He was clearly a competent hunter and an able technician, as his tool kit demonstrates. These tools, though clearly descended in principle from the preceding hand-axe cultures, were more specialized, implying that Neanderthal Man had a wider range of activities, including the processing of skin. He had learnt to use fire and practised various forms of burial, suggesting at least some conception of an after-life.

In the cave sequence of the west there appears to have been an abrupt change, not only in the tools and their method of manufacture but also in the type of hominid, for suddenly we find that modern Man had moved on to the Stone-Age stage and was replacing the Neanderthals.

This sudden disappearance of Neanderthal Man led early prehistorians to assume that these rather lowly hominids were wiped out by superior beings from the east who were not only more intelligent but possessed a superior weaponry. One prehistorian, writing in 1921, put it thus: 'Just as the early colonists in Tasmania used to organize battles, in which the unfortunate aborigines were the game, so the incoming Upper Palaeolithic people "shot at sight" whenever a Mousterian man made his appearance, until the ancient race was almost wiped out.' Yet who were these mysterious superior beings?

Some 60 years earlier, in the 1860s, a number of hominid individuals had come to light during excavations in caves which were associated with tools clearly different from those of the lowest levels. One such find came from the French village of Les Eyzies, in the Dordogne, during the construction of a railway embankment. This was the 'Old man of Cro-Magnon', one of the best preserved skulls from the French caves. The old man was not alone; there were also a woman, two other men and an unborn child, presumably the woman's. At the time of the discovery there was some doubt as to the age of the finds, as some experts could not accept that ritual burial was practised so early in human history, an interesting objection in view of the many Neanderthal burials now known.

Apart from their overall physical features, these people from Cro-Magnon showed some interesting personal details. Both the old man, who appears to have been about 50, and the woman showed signs of injury. The woman had a long cut on the side of her head which had penetrated right through the bone. There are obvious signs of healing, suggesting that she had lived for a short time afterwards. The old man had received a heavy blow on the thigh, sufficient to damage the bone without breaking it.

As well as having modern features, the Cro-Magnon people were very large individuals, with big hands and feet; burials from Grimaldi on the Italian Riviera show individuals over 1·80 metres (6 ft) in height. As well as being the apparently immediate successors of the Neanderthals, this type of advanced hominid survived until the end of the Last Glacial.

In addition to the obvious physical differences between Neanderthal Man and his successors, there were major cultural

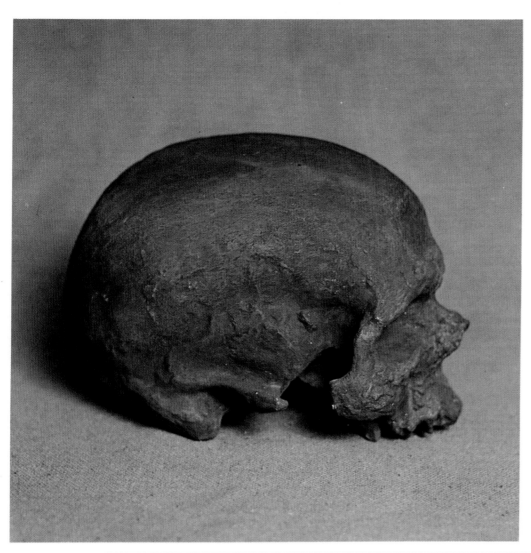

Left
The 'Old Man' from the cave of Cro-Magnon in the Dordogne is the type specimen for what has been called the Cro-Magnon race. These are clearly modern men in every way, and in none of their physical characteristics do they differ from ourselves.

The majority of these peoples are tall, 1·80 metres (6 ft), with large hands and feet. They first appeared during the interstadial between the first and second peaks of the Würm Glacial in Europe and succeeded Neanderthal Man in the French caves. Individuals of this type continued living in western Europe for the remainder of the Glaciation. In addition to living in Europe, similar populations have been found in later periods in North Africa. The old man was probably between 40 and 50 when he died, quite a good age for this period. Originally associated with the Aurignacian he is also found with the Perigordian, Solutrean and the Magdalenian.

Below
This selection of Upper Palaeolithic stone tools made by Neanderthal Man's successors do not show any major revolution in technology, but their production was more efficient and more economical, and there is a wider range of tool types suggesting more specialization.

Their improved methods of flake production included the use of a punch for detaching the flakes from the core, thus obtaining many more from the same-sized piece of raw material.

differences, both in the range of tools they used and also in the methods of their manufacture.

The basis of Mousterian technology had been the production of flakes, and it was from these that the tools were made. But the tools which succeeded them were based on a different approach. Firstly the flakes became long and narrow, blades as they are called, and more important there was a change in their method of production.

The Mousterian and earlier flake-users had produced their flakes by striking them from the core of the lump of stone with a hammer, made either of stone, or (like those for the manufacture of the well-made Acheulian hand-axes) with hammers made of wood or bone. Some of the techniques used by Neanderthal Man were very complex, but in terms of raw material they were wasteful.

The Cro-Magnon technique was based on the use of a punch in addition to the hammer stone, with the result that not only was it possible to obtain many more usable flakes from the core, but being able to place the punch in the exact position before hitting it led to far greater control. In addition to the much more efficient production of stone flakes, these people left behind them a number of tools made of either bone or antler.

Remaining in France, where the long cave sequences give a very complete idea of development during the Last Glaciation, we can see that not only are there major differences between the Mousterian and the eras that follow, there are also considerable differences in the upper part of the sequence where several different industries succeed each other.

The first of these post-Mousterian industries is named Aurignacian, after the cave at Aurignac examined by Lartet in 1861. This stage was later divided into three phases. The Lower Aurignacian, or Chatelperronian, immediately follows the Mousterian in many sites. This, the first phase of what was called the Upper Palaeolithic (the Mousterian being the Middle Palaeolithic and the hand-axe industries the Lower Palaeolithic), was not very typical of what was to follow. There were blades (some of them carefully backed), scraping tools made on the end of long blades, and what are called burins, tools which were assumed to have been used for engraving, though probably used for other purposes as well. The bone tools are few, mostly simple awls with the articulation left as part of the handle. Although classed as Upper Palaeolithic because of the production of blades and the use of bone, many of the tools are made on flakes which are indistinguishable from the earlier Mousterian.

The next stage, the original Aurignacian, is much more vigorous and the deposits much thicker. The tools are well made and there is a wide variety of types. Three things are characteristic of this stage: big blades, sometimes with large notches looking something like a modern spokeshave; small scrapers made on thick chunks of flint, some of them very beautifully made, and bone spear-points, generally slightly oval in shape. The Chatelperronian has a very limited distribution but the Aurignacian is much more widespread, occurring all over France as well as in Germany, Czechoslovakia and Austria.

It is with the Aurignacian deposits that the original Cro-Magnon skeletons were found. A further innovation in the Aurignacian is the first appearance of art. Besides the living areas, many of the Aurignacian burials have produced beads, some carved out of bone and others made from shells. While there is little doubt as to who was responsible for the Aurignacian, there are serious problems in identifying the work of the earlier Chatelperronian. In France only one burial has been found which might belong to this phase, and that is from the cave of Combe Capelle.

This site was excavated by the same man who found the burial at Le Moustier, the German dealer Hauser, and there was considerable doubt as to the relationship of the hominid to the archaeological material in the cave. Originally Combe Capelle man was thought to show marked differences from the later Cro-Magnons, and to be nearer to early *Homo sapiens* from eastern Europe. It seems now, however, that he is firmly within the range of Cro-Magnon.

The last stage of the early part of the French Upper Palaeolithic, the Gravettian, looked more like the Chatelperronian than the Aurignacian which immediately precedes it. This suggests that there were two separate groups living in France at much the same time, the Chatelperronian and Gravettian (now known as Perigordians) who have many features in common, and the Aurignacian.

Whether the differences in the two groups are due to their having belonged to two different tribes or not is uncertain, nor do we know if they lived peacefully together. Was the Aurignacian woman found at Les Eyzies attacked by a Perigordian, or were her injuries due to a family quarrel?

The next major change in the French sequence is the appearance of what is known as the Solutrean, from the site of Solutré in eastern France. In many respects the Solutrean industry does not differ greatly from what went before, many of the same tools being made by the same techniques. The difference is mainly in the class of tools, whose manufacture produced the most beautiful implements in Europe. The tools are leaf-shaped, carefully retouched on both faces, making a flat, broad, blade-like tool sometimes only 6mm. (¼ in.) thick and up to 30·5 cm. (13 in) long.

The most spectacular tools appear in the Middle Solutrean, those from the earlier stage being much smaller and generally only retouched on one face. In the last stage the points again become small and also narrower, some with the base reduced so as to form a tang. The purpose of the very large leaf-shaped tools is not very clear. In shape they suggest spearheads but they seem to be much too delicate to have served this purpose. Very similar tools are made by the Australian aborigines, though these are of glass and are very much smaller. A possible clue as to the use of these leaf-shaped tools came from a cache of 14 found buried under a rock; clearly they were someone's prized possessions, possibly ritual objects or perhaps the artifacts of a keen flint-maker showing what he could achieve.

Apart from these beautiful points, however, the rest of the Solutrean industry is not very impressive. There are scrapers and burins, but in the first two stages no backed blades; the bone industry consisted of little more than odd pieces of bone with cuts on the edges. It has been suggested that these were hunting tallies, or possibly some form of calendar. A tool which makes its appearance for the first time is the bone needle.

The last stage of the French sequence is the Magdalenian, named after La Madeleine in the Dordogne. The Magdalenian stone industry is not very impressive and many of the tools resemble those from the earlier Perigordian. It is, however, the bone and

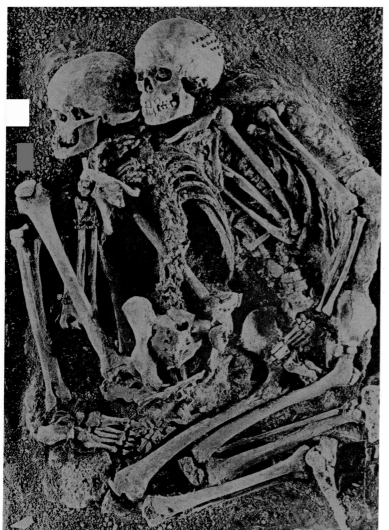

antler tools which make the period so spectacular. In the later stages the Magdalenians made harpoons with barbs, spear-throwers and many types of bone point. Many of these implements were decorated, generally with engravings of animals, and very often they were carved; it is this decoration which gives the Magdalenian its special character.

As well as caves there are many open sites known in France. One Magdalenian site in particular, Pincevent, covered a large area, the floor of which was littered with broken bones, discarded tools and waste flakes. There are also a number of hearths surrounded by stones; certain areas free of rubbish were presumably the sleeping places, and it seems that the occupants also lived in light tents.

The sequence of Upper Palaeolithic stages outlined above recurs constantly in parts of France and, though no single cave contains every stage, there are a number which have been occupied and re-occupied many times. One cave in Spain, for example, has a succession of Mousterian, Aurignacian, Solutrean and Magdalenian, and similar cave occupations existed in La Ferrassie, Laugerie Haute and the two caves at Le Moustier.

Outside western Europe, industries similar to those in France follow the local Mousterian, but there are some differences and not all the French stages are represented.

In the eastern regions of Europe, the limestone cliffs of France in which so many caves occur are largely absent. This lack of natural shelter forced Man to live in the open under whatever shelter his ingenuity could devise. Living in this area, mostly on open steppes, presented further problems, for example the lack of suitable timber. Unlike their western neighbours, the eastern Europeans primarily hunted mammoths for their meat and their ivory from which they made tools. They used mammoths' bones to form the framework for huts, the skulls and long bones making the walls and the long curved tusks the roof—the whole probably covered with either skins or turf. In addition to these mammoth houses there were lighter skin tents similar to those from the west, which were most likely intended for the summer months.

Two of the western cultures, the Solutrean and Magdalenian, are missing, though the latter penetrated as far east as Moravia and

Austria, and possibly into Poland, but not into the south Russian plains. These differences in the two parts of Europe may be due to slightly different environments, though the difference in the tools is not very marked, the later Eastern industries being so close in type to the French Gravettian that it has been called eastern Gravettian, which suggests that the hunting of different animals had little effect on the basic tool kit.

While there were few major differences in the equipment between the two areas, there are sufficient differences to suggest that the peoples were living without much direct contact. Although both the French Gravettian and that of the east manufactured small female figurines, their styles of decoration suggest that their cultures were derived from different traditions. This is also borne out by the physical appearance of the two peoples. The eastern Europeans have much more robust skulls, and well-developed brow ridges. They seem to be of a different strain from Cro-Magnon.

Who were these new Europeans? There is no possibility of the Cro-Magnons having developed directly out of the very specialized Neanderthals like those from France, but the less specialized groups of Neanderthals from the east could very well have given rise to the robust type of modern Man from eastern Europe. We have seen that the population from the caves on Mount Carmel were also extremely close to modern Man, and it is more than likely that the seeds of *Homo sapiens sapiens* were already around at least by the beginning of the Last Glaciation, if not earlier.

Outside Europe, Mousterian Man disappears at about the same time, but the industries which succeed his do not always follow the same pattern of development as those in Europe. In Africa, north of the Sahara, the local Mousterian is succeeded by industries based on the manufacture of blades by at least 34 000 B.C., but in the desert areas the Mousterian technology seems to have continued much later. South of the Sahara there is also a suggestion that the flake industries continued for much longer than in Europe, but apart from Rhodesian Man, who is roughly contemporary with the Neanderthals in Europe, we have no hominids to go with the later industries.

Across the Middle East, the Mousterian is replaced by a mixed technology with both flakes and blades, which in turn gives way to one very like the European Aurignacian. Whether this has any connection with the Aurignacian from Europe is not yet clear, but after its appearance there seems to have been no outside influence in this area and all the later industries were based on this Aurignacian. Although there were developed Neanderthals associated with a Mousterian-type industry at Mount Carmel, from one site in the same area there is a clear example of modern Man making use of the same industry.

Going further east the picture becomes very blurred. In China there is some indication of a local Mousterian, but so far no true

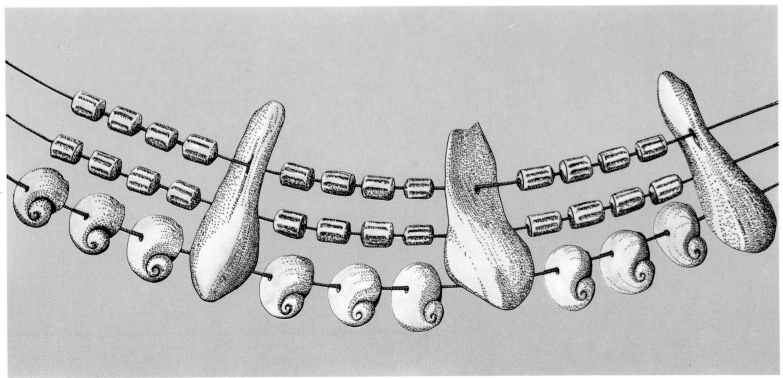

Opposite above
This type of leaf-shaped point is one of the most beautiful ever made by prehistoric Man. During the Middle Solutrean these superb examples were not very common and generally the points were both smaller and thicker, but there are enough from the living floors to suggest that examples like the one illustrated were not unusual. They were originally classed as spear points on the basis of similar, though smaller, points made by some of the Australian tribes. The best of these were made of glass or the porcelain insulators from telegraph poles. The thinness of the Solutrean tools makes them equally suitable as knives and there is one example of a broken point set into part of the jaw of a reindeer, suggesting a knife with a bone back.

Opposite below
It is not until after Neanderthal Man that we have any information regarding personal ornament, but by the beginning of the Upper Palaeolithic many pieces of jewellery occur in various forms, mostly from graves, but also many from the occupation deposits. The simplest beads are made by piercing a hole in shells, either marine shells or snails. Another simple form is made by drilling holes in the roots of teeth, mostly those of small carnivores or deer. There are even examples of human molar teeth used for this purpose.

Many very attractive beads are carved from bone, sometimes in a simple teardrop shape. There are several kinds of beads cut with a short shank so that two beads hang together. There are also examples of beads made from segments of small bones. Serving as spacers between the larger beads were fish backbones and tuskshells and, as the picture shows, many of these had very pleasing designs. The beads shown are from France.

Neanderthals have been found anywhere in the Far East, with the possible exception of Solo Man. From one of the sites at Choukoutien, the Upper Cave, came remains of what are clearly modern men with a mixed industry, but no very clear date can be given to the discovery.

Two points seem to emerge from the evidence available: firstly, the Neanderthal strain did not continue beyond about 35 000 years ago and, secondly, modern Man is certainly not derived directly from him. All one can say is that the traits which distinguished Neanderthal Man did not persist, while those of modern Man who was already on the way by the beginning of the Last Glaciation continued.

One facet of modern Man's life which has provided a great deal of information is the burial ritual, of which there is considerable evidence available. A number of the Grimaldi caves on the Italian Riviera have produced burials, some of which are very rich in personal possessions.

At the Grotte des Enfants was a double burial of a woman and a youth of about 15. The boy had four rows of shell beads on his skull, sewn on to a cap, and his mother, if that she was, had a bracelet on her wrist. Two infants from a higher level of the same cave had shells placed across their waists; these were either broad belts or the edges of tunics. A body from an adjoining cave had over 200 shells around his head and below his left knee.

The best examples of the use of beads sewn on to clothing comes from Russia, where a skeleton has been found with not only shells

on the head but all over the chest and on the legs, suggesting trousers. Two boys from a nearby grave, who were buried head to head, had similar beads as well as what appears to have been bone fastenings for their collars. Beside each boy was a spear made of ivory.

A curious custom which persisted throughout the period was the use of red ochre, an earth pigment, in the graves. Sometimes it occurs only in the form of small pieces, but elsewhere there are examples where the powdered ochre seems to have been scattered, staining the sides of the grave and the bones.

While most of the figurines depict females unclothed, there are one or two examples of the presence of clothes. A small painting of a man on a stone slab from the French cave of Angle-sur-l'Anglin shows an individual with a markedly turned-up nose who is wearing a fur coat, the collar of which seems to be of a different fur from the rest. From Buret in Siberia came a small figure wearing tunic, trousers and a hood similar to the Eskimo parka.

Taking the European Upper Palaeolithic people as a whole, they seemed content to live a life not much different from that of Neanderthal Man, but in aesthetic terms it seems to have been much richer and fuller and one can picture them living very much like the old woodland Indians of Canada, obviously content with their lot and lacking any stimulus to change. Not only was their life-style more congenial but their expectation of life had improved. Of the Neanderthals only about 1 in 20 lived to about 40, but with modern Man this had improved to about 1 in 10.

Previous page
This ivory head from a French cave is one of the most attractive pieces of prehistoric art; only about 3·5 cm high, it was probably the head of one of the many female figurines or Venuses which are well known from western Europe and as far east as Siberia. Unlike many of these figures this head, from Brassempouy in south-west France, is obviously intended as a portrait, with the face carefully carved and the hair hanging down to the shoulders. In spite of the general lack of facial features the French figures are reasonably true to life, though there are very reduced arms in some cases.

Further east the figures become very stylized and it is sometimes difficult, without the more formal examples for comparison, to be certain that they were intended to represent women at all. The purpose of these little figures is of course unknown, but in parts of Siberia, small wooden figures were kept in the huts, as charms or possibly some form of house goddess. It has been suggested that the prehistoric examples might have been fertility figures.

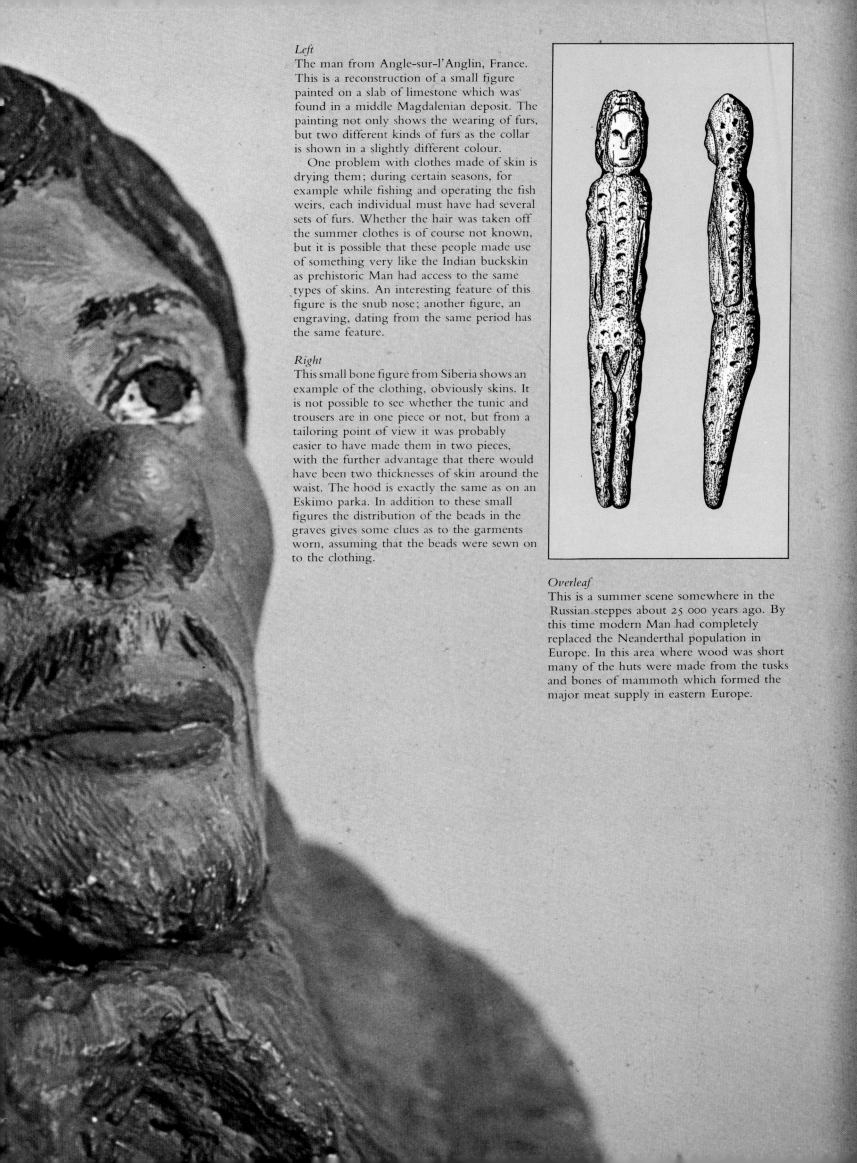

Left
The man from Angle-sur-l'Anglin, France. This is a reconstruction of a small figure painted on a slab of limestone which was found in a middle Magdalenian deposit. The painting not only shows the wearing of furs, but two different kinds of furs as the collar is shown in a slightly different colour.

One problem with clothes made of skin is drying them; during certain seasons, for example while fishing and operating the fish weirs, each individual must have had several sets of furs. Whether the hair was taken off the summer clothes is of course not known, but it is possible that these people made use of something very like the Indian buckskin as prehistoric Man had access to the same types of skins. An interesting feature of this figure is the snub nose; another figure, an engraving, dating from the same period has the same feature.

Right
This small bone figure from Siberia shows an example of the clothing, obviously skins. It is not possible to see whether the tunic and trousers are in one piece or not, but from a tailoring point of view it was probably easier to have made them in two pieces, with the further advantage that there would have been two thicknesses of skin around the waist. The hood is exactly the same as on an Eskimo parka. In addition to these small figures the distribution of the beads in the graves gives some clues as to the garments worn, assuming that the beads were sewn on to the clothing.

Overleaf
This is a summer scene somewhere in the Russian steppes about 25 000 years ago. By this time modern Man had completely replaced the Neanderthal population in Europe. In this area where wood was short many of the huts were made from the tusks and bones of mammoth which formed the major meat supply in eastern Europe.

Prehistoric Art

Our most endearing inheritance from prehistoric Man is without question his art. We can puzzle over motives, admire techniques and enjoy the flashes of impish humour which show up from time to time. But even more important, it humanizes the bones and stones, turning skeletons into people.

So far as we know, prehistoric art is an activity confined almost entirely to Europe. The rock paintings and engravings which are found throughout Africa are clearly from a later, post Glacial period.

Two categories of the European art are recognized, a division which is extremely important. The first, the mobile or home art, covers the small portable objects such as decorated tools, small carvings and paintings and engravings on small slabs of stone. The second category covers the fixed works of art, paintings, engravings and sculpture found on the walls of caves and rock shelters.

From a dating point of view this subdivision is of vital importance. Throughout the latter part of the nineteenth century a great many caves were being excavated. These excavations, particularly in the Magdalenian layers, were producing engravings and carvings of an exceptionally high standard.

Some of the earlier discoveries had been assigned to the Celtic period, but there could have been no doubt that this new material belonged to the period with which the Magdalenian were clearly associated. Many of the works of art were found together with the remains of extinct animals, and there were examples of these animals being used as the subjects too, for example the mammoth engraved on a piece of mammoth tusk, found in the Magdalenian deposits at La Madeleine.

Establishing the authenticity of the cave art was not so easy, since in most cases there was no direct archaeological association, in fact in some cases there was no archaeological material in the cave at all; further, many of the caves were open and anyone could have had access at any period.

That the early supporters of the antiquity of cave art had immense problems of this kind is shown by the fate of the Marquis of Sautuala. The Marquis, a keen prehistorian, was excavating the cave of Altamira in northern Spain and found in one of the chambers a magnificent ceiling covered with red bison. His claim that these paintings were of the same age as the deposits he was excavating was met with complete derision by most of his contemporaries. They even went so far as to accuse him of having hired an artist from Madrid to paint them. The poor Marquis was not vindicated until after his death. The fact that many of the animals shown were extinct, such as the mammoth and rhinoceros, was no help as their presence in the cave deposits was, of course, common knowledge to the educated public, so accusations of forgery could not be refuted.

The French prehistorian, Piette, was largely responsible for the changes of opinion. His excavations were producing works of art whose various styles were so close to those on the cave walls that it was becoming difficult to support the idea of forgery, and by the beginning of the present century most prehistorians were prepared to accept this aspect of prehistoric Man's culture.

What finally convinced the doubters was the discovery of wall decorations covered by undisturbed archaeological deposits, proving that they were far older than the deposits which covered them.

The first examples of prehistoric art come from the early part of the Upper Palaeolithic, beginning roughly about 30 000 and continuing to around 10 000 years ago. This dating depends, of course, on survival and also on what one means by art. Colouring matter in the form of red ochre has been recorded from Acheulian deposits in Africa and manganese black is known from Mousterian deposits in France. These natural pigments were readily available and easy to prepare and one must assume that they had been used for body paint from a very early period; it is also reasonable to suppose that there was some painting of wood and possibly leather.

It is not until the early part of the Upper Palaeolithic that any art objects have survived. Some rather crude engravings and paintings relating to the Aurignacian have been found in France, for example from La Ferrassie. One or two of the subjects are instantly recognizable, such as the rhinoceros, but others are vague. There have been suggestions that some of these obscure signs are female sex symbols, which are well documented in their later appearances.

From this rather simple beginning to the later complex figurines, or Venuses as they are called, is a big step. These small figures, made in a variety of materials (stone, bone, ivory or clay) show great variety and skill, though generally they are rather stylized.

In France these figurines are associated with the later stages of the Perigordian, and spread across into eastern Europe, occurring in Czechoslovakia, Austria and even on the south Russian steppes, the most easterly coming from Siberia. Despite this enormous area of distribution, all the figures have two features in common; no face is ever sculpted, yet the breasts and buttocks are generally accentuated.

One of the best known of the figurines is the Venus of Willendorf in Austria. The lady, carved in stone, is generously proportioned, in fact she is distinctly fat; the hands, which are very small, are resting on the breasts; the hair is shown as a series of rings, but no attempt is made to show the face and the feet are missing.

A slightly different version of the Venus figure comes from Laussel in France. This is also a generous figure, but, unlike the majority of other figurines is a limestone relief, probably originally carved on the wall but found detached. Like the lady from Willendorf, she too is given hair, but no face, and she is portrayed holding a bison horn in her right hand. Slightly earlier than these Venuses are a group of small ivory animals from an Aurignacian cave in Germany.

Whether the figurines originated in eastern or western Europe, or occurred spontaneously in both is uncertain, since the available dates (between 29–25 000 B.C.) cover both areas.

The Solutrean, which followed the Perigordian stage, has produced engraved limestone plaques of animals, many of them so covered with lines as to be almost obliterated. At one site in the département of Charante, Le Roc del Ser, was found what appears to have been part of a frieze made up of stone blocks. A number of these portray animals carved in relief, one in particular showing a little man being chased by a bison.

These stone blocks were found between two Solutrean layers and, although the site also contains Perigordian layers, they are generally attributed to the Solutrean. In addition to the engravings there are simple carvings from Solutrean sites in the Dordogne, of

Left
The interest of this rather late example of Magdalenian engraving lies in the fact that it was one of the earliest examples of prehistoric art to be found. This piece, showing two hinds, from one of the caves at Chaffaud in the département of Vienne in France, was found some time between 1834 and 1845. It is now not certain what was found with this piece of reindeer bone, but it was originally described as 'celtic' in an 1864 publication called the 'Antediluvian and Celtic period in Poitou'.

Above
This object was found by Lartet at La Madeleine between 1863 and 1864. If ever confirmation for prehistoric art was needed this would seem to have been all that was required. From the remains of almost complete mammoths found in the frozen grounds in Siberia we now know a great deal about this animal and the accuracy of this drawing is remarkable. The artist obviously had a very intimate knowledge of the creature, which is shown by the execution of the very characteristic domed head and the long sweeping tusks. In spite of this clear evidence for the antiquity of the art it took a long time for the cave paintings to be finally attributed to the people who had created them.

Left
The majority of the Australian tribes painted caves, personal possessions and themselves. This particular group of paintings in the Northern Territory shows animals such as kangaroo and crocodile, as well as apparent abstracts and what seems to represent a river.

The Bushman of the Kalahari desert were painting in rock shelters up to the end of the last century and paintings which probably belonged to them several thousand years ago occur in parts of East Africa. The motives underlying these paintings seem to differ.

Many of those from Australia are concerned with tribal legend and seem to have little connection with either sympathetic hunting magic or the recording of events.

71

the type found at Solutré and in the French Pyrenees. In the late Solutrean deposits at Parpallo, in southern Spain, there are both engravings and paintings of animals on limestone slabs.

It is not until the middle of the Magdalenian that the home art reaches a truly high standard. The early stages produce very little of importance except that here begins the tradition of engraving on bones and antler tools. In the first two of the six stages of the Magdalenian the decoration of tools is very simple, little more than abstract designs with a few rather simple animal heads. In stage three there are abstract designs arranged in geometric patterns as well as examples of carving on the larger implements.

There is no question that the peak of the home art is in the next two stages, IV and V. Here the carving reaches a high degree of craftsmanship, particularly in Magdalenian IV. In addition to excellent carvings, many of the tools are engraved with various animal designs, and are frequently lightly sketched and well-drawn. In the last stage there is a noticeable decline, the carving disappears altogether and the engraving becomes very wooden and uninspired. This decline is difficult to understand as the tools themselves are better made and more efficient than in the preceding stages.

What seems to have triggered off the carving in the first place seems to have been the use of larger bone and antler tools, principally the spear-thrower, an implement used by the Australian aborigines to increase the range of their spears. The heavy versions of the Palaeolithic throwers made use of a lump of bone or antler left at the end, presumably to act as a weight, and it is this area which frequently received the attentions of the carvers. Sometimes the whole implement is carved in the form of an animal, some part of which, the tail for example, forms the hook.

In addition to these functional pieces, there are many small pieces of carving which seem to have been executed for their own sake, like the beautiful head of a horse found in the French Pyrenees. A rather curious find came from a cave in the Dordogne: this was a cache of limestone plaques engraved with animals, which were in far greater quantity than usual in Magdalenian deposits. This has been interpreted either as forming part of an artist's studio or even an art school.

Looking at the home art as a whole, as far as France is concerned, there is a steady development from the Aurignacian to the Magdalenian, the main progress being in a general improvement in the drawing and later the carving. Nowhere is there a major break in development, whether in technique or subject matter to suggest any important outside influences.

The later stages of the Magdalenian penetrated into the fringes of eastern Europe where quite typical Magdalenian engravings have been found, but this late intrusion does not seem to have had any influence on the eastern art as a whole. This area, with its rather simple geometric designs and stylized human figures, seems to have developed largely independently though possibly it was the originator of the later art in Siberia.

Following the development of cave art is not as easy as with home art, owing to the general lack of direct archaeological association. It is in this area that style plays an important part.

A good example of this comes from northern Spain. During excavations at the cave of Altamira, a shoulder blade was found on which was engraved the head of a hind. The importance of this find was not in the engraving itself but rather in the unusual technique employed, the face and the front part of the neck being accentuated by vertical lines; the date of this piece was early Magdalenian. On the wall of the cave of Castillo not far away was the engraved head of a hind executed in exactly the same technique, so close in fact are the two that it seems probable that they were done by the same person, thus the date for one would apply to the other.

Further help comes from the habit of one artist making a painting or engraving on top of a previous one, producing what is called superposition. It has been possible in some cases to work out the order in which the paintings were executed, thus giving some idea as to the succession of styles. Lastly, there are incidences of where paintings or engravings have been covered by datable archaeological deposits. This unfortunately only gives the latest possible date, not the earliest.

Correlating the cave art with the known stages of French Upper Palaeolithic history is not very precise and few prehistorians would be prepared to claim more than two or three recognizable cycles,

two being generally accepted: Aurignacian/Perigordian and Solutrean/Magdalenian.

The early part of the first cycle starts with simple finger tracing in the clay surface of the cave walls; much of this is meanders but there are examples of simple animal drawings, mostly of oxen. Possibly a little later are animals outlined in paint and engravings cut rather deeply into the cave wall. A good example of these engravings comes from the cave of Pair-non-Pair in southern France. These engravings are just above an Aurignacian deposit and are covered by late Perigordian, allowing a fairly accurate date to be placed on them. The animals are rather crudely drawn and emerge out of a tangle of seemingly unrelated lines. The drawings, though simple, are well-observed and well executed but the lines are rather thick.

An apparent development of the outline paintings is animal paintings executed in flat wash, and in this style there are some very nice examples of oxen and horses, the latter having strangely pointed faces.

In the second cycle, the Solutrean/Magdalenian, there are obvious advances in execution. How much of this can be attributed to the Solutreans is uncertain, as there is very little of their mobile art available for comparison. It has recently been suggested that some of the painted caves which have been attributed to the late Perigordian may in reality belong to the Solutrean.

The most developed of the art forms clearly belongs to the Magdalenian, and it is to this period that the superb painted ceiling of Altamira belongs. The changes seen in the later stages are largely a matter of improvement in execution, but there are many examples of the increasing use of colour tone for shading. This technique greatly improves the sense of depth and one would assume that it grew out of the understanding of form learnt from the use of carving in the home art. The high level of draftsmanship shown by the painters is shared by the engravings some of which, considering that they were done by stone tools, are astonishingly fluid.

An unusual medium to have survived is modelling in clay. It is reasonable to suppose that clay figure modelling had been continuing since the beginning of primitive Man's existence and there are examples of small clay animals from Czechoslovakia, which have survived because they were slightly baked. The most impressive example of clay modelling comes from the French Pyrenees where, in the deep recesses of a cave, two clay bisons were found leaning against a rock. There are other examples of clay animals in the same region, but not so well preserved.

European cave art is very regional: most is in south-west France and near the northern coast of Spain, with outliers to the south. East of this area, cave art is almost non-existent, only re-appearing occasionally in the Russian Urals. This rather strange distribution is probably geological rather than cultural, and it is only the exceptional limestone caves of the west which have preserved the art. The hunters of the eastern steppes had no suitable caves to live in let alone paint in, though there are examples of painting on the mammoth bones of the houses.

Up to now we have been discussing primitive art in terms of technique and development. The most important aspect of all is of course the subject matter. It is the animals which dominate the choice of subject. Reindeer, horse, ox and bison are depicted most frequently. However, nearly all the animals whose remains have been found in cave deposits are included, though the carnivores, such as lions, bears and wolves are in the minority. The mammoth and rhinoceros, which play little part in the later economy, are nevertheless drawn and painted and the mammoth is also depicted in carvings. Vegetation is rare and there are few examples of plants.

A curious feature is the part humans play in the art. With very few exceptions the human form is denied the care lavished on the animals, so that most of them can only be described as caricatures. They appear on the home art as well as on the cave walls as strange little figures obviously playing a very subordinate role. Some are dressed or disguised in animal skins; for example, the well-known figures of the 'sorcerer' from the Pyrenees—a human figure in the skin of a reindeer with the antlers on his head.

Unlike the later paintings from eastern Spain and Africa there is no suggestion of composition. With one or two possible exceptions the animals are alone, so that instead of painting a scene of, say, horses in a landscape, the artist seems to have been content to

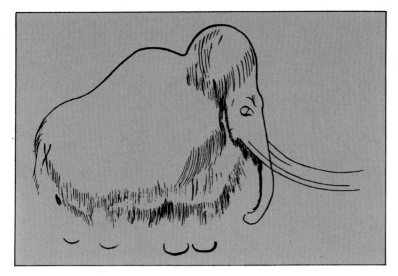 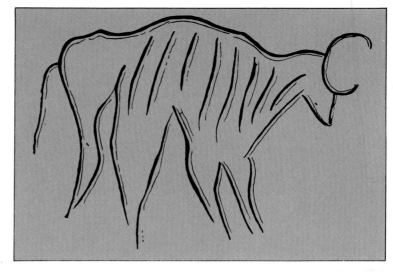

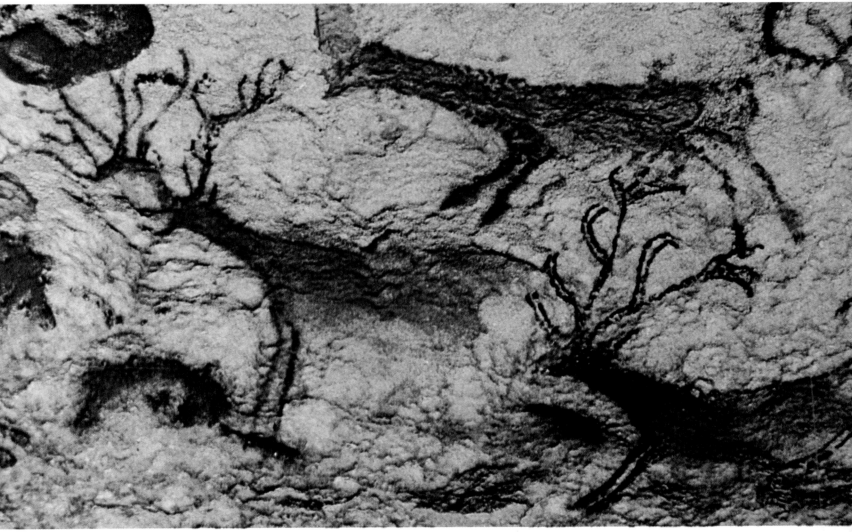

Top left
Like the mammoth from La Madeleine this is an engraving, but in this case on the wall of a cave. The characteristic outline of the animal is as sharply drawn as in the first one, and it has a rather nice technique for showing the feet. The long reddish hair, which is known from the Siberian frozen mammoths, is clearly shown as indeed are the domed forehead and the long tusks. Although the mammoth does not seem to have played so important a part in the diet of the western Upper Palaeolithic people, it was the staple diet of those in the eastern plains.

Top right
These designs done with the finger in the clay of a cave floor in Spain have survived because the clay has become hardened. Probably much of the very early art, such as drawing and modelling, was done in clay; much of this of course failed to survive.

These clay drawings are attributed to the Aurignacian on the grounds of style. The method of depicting horns in a different plane from the rest of the animal is known from some of the early examples of home art, and this twisted perspective continues throughout most of the first cycle of the art.

Above
A group of red deer painted on the wall of the cave of Lascaux, south-west France, which was a very popular tourist attraction until it was found necessary to close it to the public owing to the deterioration of the paintings.

Originally dated to the Perigordian, the cave contains red deer, small horses and a number of large oxen; the absence of the reindeer suggests an Interstadial date for the paintings. It has recently been suggested that some of this work should be attributed to the Solutrean, a period which in the past has been thought to be almost lacking in cave art. Some of the animals, such as the deer, appear to have all been painted at the same time and seem to represent a herd.

produce one isolated animal. Further, there is the feeling that the drawing of this single animal was sufficient in itself, even the position and relation to anything else on the wall seems to have been of little importance. It did not seem to matter that some of the drawing was not even horizontal. This rather detached approach is odd: there must have been so many incidents in a hunter's life which could have been the subject of graphic representations.

In all the stages, though more so in the later ones, the artists obviously had a thorough knowledge of the animals of their time, and those which are still with us, such as the horse and reindeer, are so accurately drawn that we can have considerable confidence in early Man's drawing of extinct species such as the mammoth and woolly rhinoceros. We are familiar with the appearance of these from the frozen mammoths found in Siberia and the complete rhinoceros discovered in a pitch lake in Romania.

The great care expended on the animals makes it very frustrating that the humans have been denied the same treatment. It would have been fascinating to have had real portraits of our early ancestors. One personal touch we do have though is provided by pictures of hands. These were executed either by the artist's hand being placed against the wall and the outline being painted, or by dipping the hand into paint and pressing it against the wall.

We are not absolutely certain as to all the techniques used, but some of them have recently been successfully duplicated. The pigments are red and yellow ochre, a natural earth colouring; manganese or carbon producing black, and china clay giving white. A number of stone slabs have been found which were used for grinding the paint, and from one site hollow bones were discovered which contained red ochre. It is not certain whether the paint was used as water colour or mixed with fat, but the general state of preservation suggests the latter. It was applied with the fingers, or with brushes made of chewed sticks or possibly simple brushes made of fur. Some of the paint seems to have been blown through a tube, as in the case of the negative hand prints.

What were the motives behind this art? Ever since its recognition, prehistorians have been searching for an answer. As the art itself provides none it is necessary to turn to the modern hunting communities in search of motives. One suggestion which has received support for many years is that the paintings represent some form of hunting magic. By creating the image of a particular animal the man attempts to ensure success in his hunting through a form of sympathetic magic, such as that practised by some American Indians.

Such an idea might explain the paintings of single animals the representation of which was vitally important to early Man. Since its function was primarily short term, it could be drawn anywhere that was convenient. This might also explain why the paintings are found in the back of the caves which never saw the light of day and must have been executed in very poor artificial light.

Were these dark recesses, however, sanctuaries where secret hunting rituals were practised? Some prehistorians have seen the animals as being totems, either tribal or personal. Others have suggested pure decoration, which is unlikely in view of their location, while others have claimed a motive no more complex than 'art for art's sake'.

When considering any of these possibilities several factors must be borne in mind. All the various representations found cover some 20 000 years, at least in Europe, and span several industrial traditions whose inter-relationships are unknown. Also, are the motives the same for both the home and the cave art? The urge to decorate one's possessions is certainly strong enough without needing to evoke deep magico-religious motives, though carving an animal on one's spear-thrower might suggest some optimism.

Yet once one has visited the French and Spanish caves it becomes impossible to deny a very strong motive indeed. Some caves like Niaux in the Pyrenees contain paintings and engravings located fairly distant from the entrance, a difficult journey even with modern lighting. One can imagine the hours spent chipping out the frieze of animals from Le Roc del Ser or the 1·50 metre- (5 ft-) long horses carved on the wall at Cap Blanc; these works of art were never the result of mere whim.

Whatever the motives, prehistoric Man was a great artist by any standards. His technical skills reached great heights and, looking at the best of his productions, one can deny him neither the claims of 'skill for skill's sake' nor 'art for art's sake'.

Above
This painting of a bison from the ceiling of the cave of Altamira in northern Spain became the celebrated first example of what was claimed to be prehistoric cave art and was originally treated with ridicule. The site, in addition to the paintings and engravings, contained rich Solutrean and Magdalenian occupation deposits, though the art covers a wider range than this. There is no question that these paintings are the most sophisticated in prehistoric art.

Two factors make these paintings outstanding: one is the richness of the colour and the other is the use of tone variation as a means of indicating modelling, in this case black was used in conjunction with the red. Attempts to show the essential curves of the animals are well known in both engraving and painting, except for the simple outlines and some of the early flatwash paintings. In many of the fine line engravings, the contours are indicated by stressing the growth of the hair, and this is also done by fine lines in some of the paintings.

Above right top
The Venus of Willendorf is probably the best known of the Upper Palaeolithic figurines. Found in an Eastern Gravettian layer in an open site in Austria it epitomizes the general trends of these figures. To say that the lady was overweight would be an understatement since she is in fact extremely fat. It is interesting that this is not an attempt to show what a fat women would look like; it is a portrait of a fat woman, with every other part of her except the arms in perfect proportion. These small Venuses have sometimes been referred to as fertility figures, such as are known in the later farming communities; but this seems unlikely.

Above right
This engraving on a small piece of bone implies a sense of humour in the otherwise rather serious art. The bison, of which only the head remains intact, has been dismembered, the fore limbs lying on the ground. The whole of the body has disappeared leaving only the back bone. Whether the scene is intended to

commemorate a banquet or shows the diversion of a kill according to the rules of precedent is uncertain.

The dividing of game carcases into clearly determined portions according to status is well known among hunting communities, but it is difficult to see how this particular bison was divided. Where, for example, is the meat from the trunk? Was it stripped from the bone and carried away, or have the seven diners eaten their way through the complete body? The evidence from the cave deposits suggests that not all of the kill was brought back to camp, and there is some evidence that the backbone is frequently missing, while the limb bones and parts of the head are well represented. One explanation for this scene is that the movable meat has been stripped off and the remainder left. If this interpretation is correct it would imply that there was a fair amount of game available. It is possible that the four objects in the bottom right-hand corner may represent bows.

Overleaf
A magnificent bison from the cave of Font de Gaume in the Dordogne. The technique employed is very similar to that of the bison from Altamira. Here, however, the artist has taken some liberties and has accentuated some features such as the heavy shoulders and the mass of hair on the chest, making what is almost a caricature; nevertheless, it has been beautifully executed.

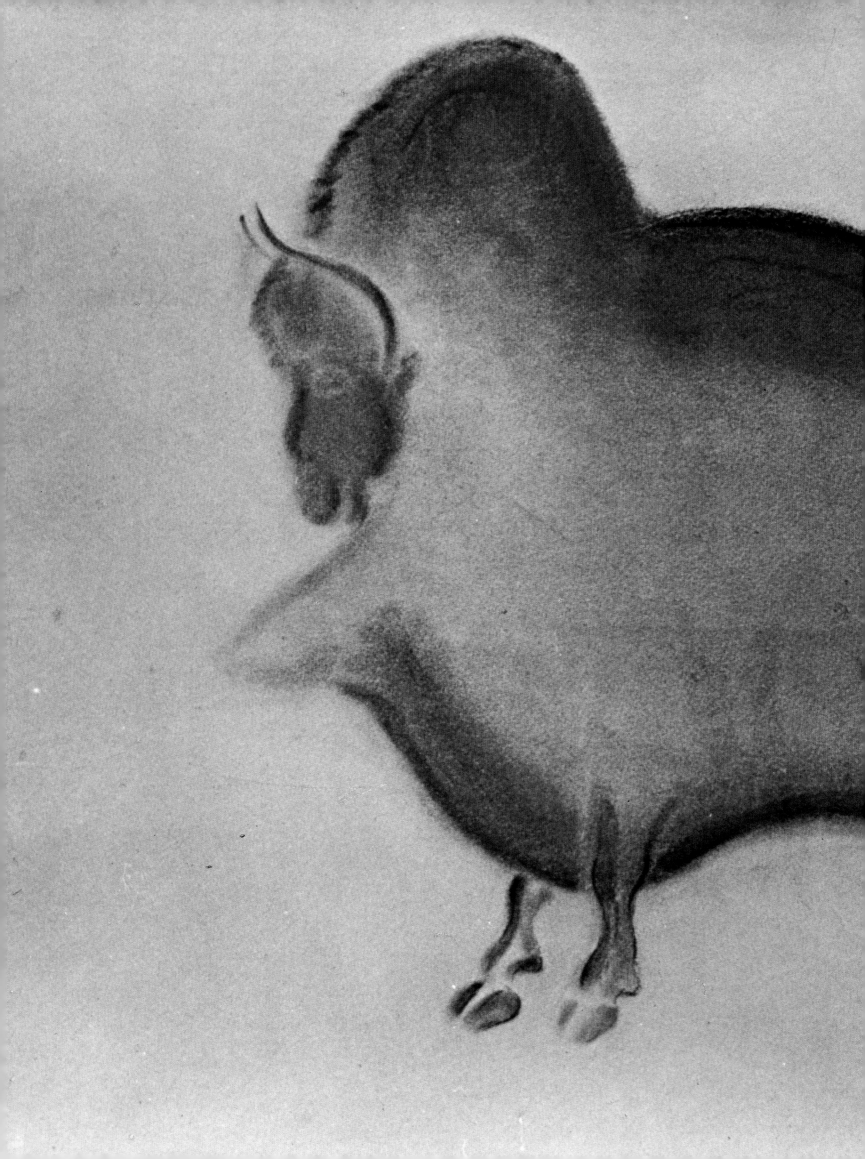

Below right
Judging from the complete body of a woolly rhinoceros found in a pitch lake in Romania, this painting in red from the cave of Font de Gaume is accurate, the shape and hang of the head being well observed. Although based on outline the work is very sophisticated. The general contours are outlined by very skilful use of the shaggy coat, and the whole is beautifully proportioned.

This painting has been dated to the Perigordian but the advanced approach suggests that it is later, probably Magdalenian. In view of the very high standards of many of the paintings and engravings one wonders whether there were in fact specialist artists. If art played an important part in the lives of Upper Palaeolithic Man, possibly associated with some form of magic, then it is not unreasonable to suppose that there were groups of wise men, witch doctors, or shamen, who were responsible for the ritual aspects and whose standing depended not only on the results obtained by their magic, but on the standard of their drawing.

Below
These engravings of two hinds' heads are important as that on the shoulder blade came from a sealed archaeological deposit in the cave of Altamira, and is Magdalenian. The second on the wall of the Castillo cave, not far away, is almost identical. As this particular technique of engraving is unusual it is reasonable to suppose that both were executed at the same time, possibly by the same person, and thus the date of the wall engraving would also be Magdalenian.

Opposite page, left
Unlike many of the female figurines, the Venus of Laussel is a relief carved in limestone. It was probably carved on the wall of the shelter, though it was found detached, covered with Perigordian deposits.

In general concept it resembles the Venus of Willendorf very closely.

Unlike the majority of these figures this one is holding something in her hand, a bison horn. Laussel also differs from Willendorf in regard to the hair, one being shown with tight curls and the other with the hair flowing over the shoulders.

Many of the figurines are shown with what appears to be an excess of fat around the buttocks, and some prehistorians have suggested that this is an accumulation of reserve fat, similar to that seen on some Bushman women. Looking at these figures as a whole it seems more likely that in trying to emphasize the female character the artist has overdone certain aspects.

Opposite page, right
Cut on the curved surface of a piece of bone, the proportions of this Upper Palaeolithic carving are of a high order and the hairy texture of the head is indicated by pitting over the whole surface. The back of the bone is left blank. There are many examples of these small carvings, some are part of a tool like the heads of some spear throwers, but some seem to have been done

for their own sake. One site in southern France has produced a series of small bone silhouettes of chamois heads. Their use is uncertain.

While there is a strong case for considering that much of Upper Palaeolithic art had a serious purpose, it is necessary also to consider the possibility of art for art's sake, and there must have been long periods during the year, particularly in the winter, when there was a great deal of spare time.

Opposite page, below
This group of antler tools, from La Madeleine are late Magdalenian and show clearly the rather wooden appearance due to the deeply cut lines, which cost the artist his freedom of line. The tools on which these drawings are applied are made on the main beam of the antler. At the wide part, where the brow tine branches off, is a hole. A number of these tools have come down from the Magdalenian and their purpose is unknown. Various suggestions have been put forward: that they were for straightening arrows, that they were used for reaming leather thongs, that they were drum sticks, or even ceremonial batons.

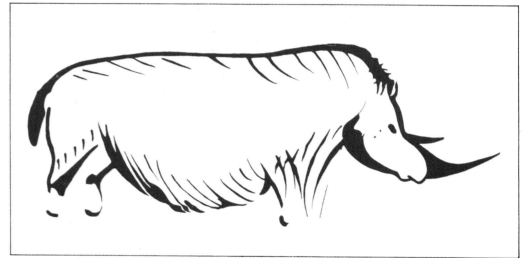

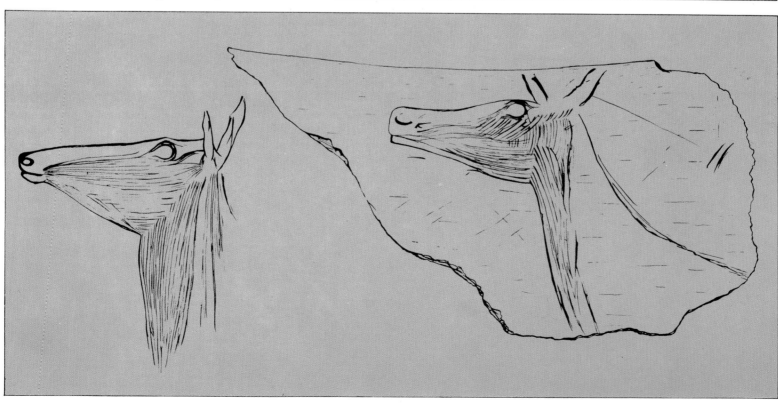

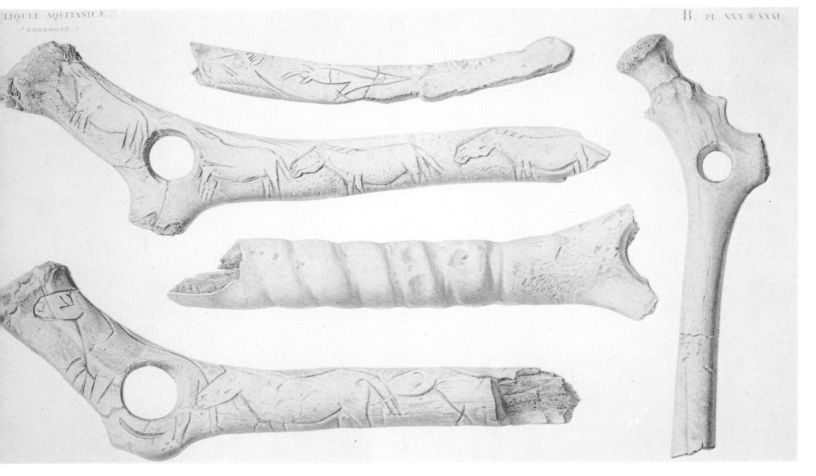

Primitive Hunting

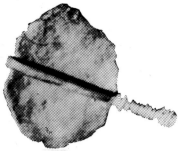

In the same way that we turned to modern hunting and food-gathering communities for clues about the motives involved in prehistoric Man's art, so we must also depend on present-day tribal communities to broaden our understanding of the actual life-style of early Man.

But this cannot be taken to extremes. For many years, for example, it was fashionable to make direct comparisons with modern peoples supposedly living in the same type of environment as early man. On the assumption that the Last Glaciation gave rise to arctic conditions, the Upper Palaeolithic was naturally compared with the Arctic tundra and its occupants with the Eskimos, particularly those whose economy largely depended on the migratory caribou, the American form of reindeer.

The Upper Palaeolithic peoples, particularly the Magdalenians, certainly had many tools in common with the inland Caribou Eskimos and their seal-hunting cousins on the coasts. And this led to the over-simplified view based on the notion that prehistoric Man was merely the European equivalent of the Eskimo, living in the same climate, using the same tools to hunt the same animals, and even, according to some, having much the same skull shape. Some prehistorians even went so far as to suggest that the Eskimos are the last of the Magdalenians who followed the retreating reindeer eastwards after the end of the Last Glaciation. Better understanding of the climates of the Last Glaciation have emphasized the need for a more cautious consideration not only of the basic Magdalenian-Eskimo comparison, but of all comparisons with any modern tribal group.

Where the comparative argument is flawed is in trying to transform it into concrete form. The evidence on the ground does not confirm the theory. To the south of the Loire, at the main sites of palaeolithic occupation of France, the conditions were simply never comparable to the Arctic tundra, though from about 29–16 000 B.C. the area was very cold, with some improvement occurring during the interstadials. Unpleasant as these conditions might have been, life was never as rigorous as in the northern tundra. There was never a complete absence of trees for fuel, there were many very good caves for shelter and the region was abundant in game, which alone makes the comparison even less valid.

The Eskimos on the other hand were entirely dependent on the migrating caribou for food and without these animals the economy would have collapsed completely–for they depended on the caribou not only for their food, but also for their clothing, bedding and tents. The bones and antlers were used for tools, as well as for the Eskimos' composite bows and strings.

While there is no doubt that the Upper Palaeolithic peoples depended on hunting to more or less the same extent they had, in addition to the reindeer, herds of horses, bison, and oxen to choose from, plus a wider range of fur-bearing animals. And far from living in arctic conditions the European Upper Palaeolithic men lived a life nearer to that of the American Indians, particularly those who lived where the forest and tundra meet.

Although we have no direct evidence as to how prehistoric Man hunted, by reviewing the various methods known to us, we can at least get some idea of the techniques available to early Man. Primitive hunting generally takes two forms: either individual

hunting, where one man or a very small group work on their own, or communal hunting in which the whole family, or in some cases combinations of neighbouring families take an active part.

Leaving aside scavenging (probably man's main source of meat) hunting can be divided into several categories: direct attack, driving and trapping. The first involves cornering an animal, attacking young or weak members of a herd; this calls for stalking skills of a high order or, alternatively, some forms of ambush. The requirements are a deep knowledge of the animals being hunted, and great experience of tracking.

Several modern groups use a variety of disguises in order to approach the heard without alarming it. There is a picture by the American artist Catlin showing two Indians wearing wolf-skins creeping up on a herd of bison. A very attractive Bushman painting in South Africa shows a hunter wearing an ostrich skin and insinuating himself into a group of very suspicious ostriches.

Good stalking, which forms the basis of Bushman hunting, allows the hunter to get extremely close to a herd. Sometimes animals can be lured into an ambush by imitation of either a mating call or the lowing of a calf. The American Indians employ this technique with great success in the forests, making moose calls out of bark. Bird calls are a variation on this idea, and the use of captive decoy birds is often extremely successful.

Any form of direct confrontation naturally requires efficient hunting equipment. From very early times spears seem to have formed the main weapon for most forms of hunting. The spears were probably originally made with a fire-hardened tip like the yew spear from the Clactonian site at Clacton, or the lighter version found in association with the bones of an elephant from a site in Germany, probably dating from the Last Interglacial. These simple spears would have been very efficient and there are examples of Australian and New Guinea spears skilfully barbed and carved out of single pieces of wood.

It seems fairly certain that the triangular Mousterian points were hafted as spear heads in a similar way to those from the Admiralty Islands and parts of Australia. The stone spear heads of the Australians are attached to the shaft by a form of vegetable adhesive, but could equally well have been bound on with sinew, as are most modern projectile heads.

Apart from spears the bow and arrow play a very large part in modern hunting, as they once did in war. The simplest form of bow ever devised was a single piece of wood; but where wood was short, as with the Eskimos and the Mongolian Tartars, very effective bows were made of bone plates lashed together.

The Upper Palaeolithic bone points were obviously intended for some hostile use, as were the flint points with a tang from the earlier Perigordian, Solutrean and the late Magdalenian. The art, however, provides us with no conclusive drawing of a bow or arrows in use. The one possible exception are some engraved Perigordian pebbles which show animals with what look like feathered arrows sticking into their sides. Since we know of spear throwers in the late Magdalenian, it must be concluded that spears played some part; deductions made from modern comparisons on this point only serve to throw the whole question into great confusion. To make matters worse, the Australians use the spear thrower but not the bow, while the Eskimos use both spear and

Above
Two Eskimos fishing through ice in Alaska. This type of winter fishing is quite profitable and is a way of varying the winter diet. Seals are also caught through breathing holes, and the hunters sometimes make a scratcher of seal claws which, when rubbed on the edge of the ice, attracts the seal.

Various small lures are also made to attract the seal to the hole where it is then speared. For this purpose a detachable barbed harpoon head is used and the wounded seal played on a line after spearing. Some of the Magdalenian barbed points have a hole at the base which might have served for the line, though there is no evidence of a prehistoric coastal economy like that of the Eskimos.

Overleaf
The Eskimo tribes living on the coast derived most of their meat from the sea mammals, such as the walrus. These animals also provided excellent quality furs and blubber which, when rendered down, provided oil for lamps, cooking and heating. Sometimes when hunting on ice the Eskimos used a low white screen pushed along in front of them as camouflage.

In addition to land hunting much of their game was taken in the sea from kayaks which were also used for killing reindeer as they swam across rivers. All short-range hunting requires some form of stalking, but it is unlikely that Palaeolithic Man did much of this during the winter as crossing the snow even with snow shoes would have been difficult.

One winter activity that was most frequently undertaken was trapping, since animal prints in the snow clearly showed game trails. It was during the coldest winter months that the fur was at its best and both the Arctic fox and hare as well as the ermine all had white fur coats.

Right

Lake Rudolf is the site of many of the recent finds of early Man and this gives some idea of what it must have been like nearly 3 million years ago. Fishing seems to have played a part in the diet from very early times and the inhabitants of the lake at Olduvai caught and ate large quantities of cat-fish.

These Turkanas are using a circular trap made of local reeds; such traps were probably used by most prehistoric peoples and many modern varieties are known. Sometimes the traps are baited, sometimes just set in a channel through which the fish pass. Various forms of weirs are also constructed, particularly useful with fish like salmon which migrate in large numbers.

Far right

An Australian hunter returning after a hunt. Of particular interest is the spear thrower he is carrying in his hand. This is a bigger example than usual but the hook at the end can be clearly seen. This is the same weapon as those found in middle and late Magdalenian deposits in France and these were most likely used in the same way.

Though requiring a great deal of practice, spear throwers make a considerable difference to how far a spear can actually be hurled.

Like those of the Eskimos, the Magdalenian spearthrowers are short; straight pieces of antler were in short supply but there is a possibility that some were attached to a wooden shaft.

bow, but only use the spear thrower for small game and their throwers are much smaller in size.

For the larger animals, like the mammoth, the digging of deep pits would appear to have been the answer, and there are several modern examples of pit-ambushing techniques. There is an 18th century German engraving showing a file of elephants marching into a pit, in this case with a sharpened stake at the bottom.

Such pits could be dug with simple digging sticks of the kind used by many peoples for getting up roots and digging animals out of their burrows. The driving of large game animals into swampy ground seems to have been practised from very early times, and we know of definite examples of elephants being hunted by the hand-axe makers in Spain and even earlier at Olduvai.

Another possible hunting technique employed by early Man was to chase small game on foot. Man is capable of running extremely fast over a short distance and we have already mentioned following the herds to pick off the young and the weak, though in Africa one might find lions doing the same thing and not being very concerned whether the game or their fellow hunters end up between their jaws. It is even possible for a group of hunters to imitate the methods of the hunting dogs and wear the game down simply by keeping it on the move.

Driving game on to concealed hunters or into some sort of pen is also a practical method with herd animals, though it usually requires a large number of people, and a high level of organization, and in this even very young children can help by taking a part. The American Indians sometimes drove bison into pens entered through wide funnels made of timber walling. The Eskimos used a similar technique to catch reindeer, using piles of stones or 'dead men' erected at intervals to form the funnel. Another variant was to drive the herds over cliffs. This was wasteful but effective, particularly when the meat could be either dried or frozen for future use. At Solutré the late Perigordians drove horses over the cliffs. During excavations at the base, the remains of over 20 000 horses were found. The Indians, using snow shoes, also drove bison into deep snow where they became helpless.

Trapping, particularly of fur animals, must have been common

and the same methods were available for food animals as well. Traps could have been in the form of either snares set across game trails and suitable for small game and ground birds such as partridge, or fall traps for the bigger animals.

In addition to their primary role in supplying food, many animals were a valuable source of raw material. Reindeer supplied fur, bison and red deer provided clothing and bedding as well as tent material; bones and antlers were used for many tools (mammoth ivory extensively used in eastern Europe is an example of this application). Leather for thongs, bags, water carriers and sinew for attaching heads to spears, and teeth for necklaces are just a few of the many uses to which the animals were put. As with most of the fur-covered peoples in northern Europe and America, some furs were used for their appearance as well as their utility, such as fox and weasel furs. The fur of the wolverine or glutton was prized by the Eskimo for lining the opening of the parka hood when it was found that snow did not freeze on it. Finally the fat of all the animals was undoubtedly rendered down to provide the fuel for the Magdalenian stone lamps.

The Mousterians seem to have killed large numbers of the huge cave bear and the rhinoceros, numerous skulls of which have been found in several caves in Switzerland and elsewhere. It has been suggested that there was some kind of ritual attached to these skulls but this cannot be proved. It seems curious that they should have wanted to keep such bulky objects in their caves.

In addition to the cave bear, fossil remains of the smaller brown bear and the cave lion have been found among the cave deposits, as well as being depicted in wall paintings and on carved objects. Whether they were killed for their skins or perhaps as a test of manhood, as with the modern Masai, is not known.

While the bulk of the meat diet seems to have been obtained from the large game animals, fish were also eaten at least during the European Upper Palaeolithic. Many bones of salmon and trout have been found and there are a number of fish depicted in both the home and cave art. How they were caught is uncertain, but traps could have been set in channels, or weirs built to intercept river or migratory fish. Fish-trapping was a pursuit in which the

whole family would have taken part. This haul of fish was most likely dried or smoked and would have been used to eke out the rather poor summer supply of fresh meat. In addition to trapping, barbed harpoons of the late Magdalenian were suitable for use as fish spears and are almost identical to those still used in many parts of the world.

As well as fishing, Cro-Magnon would have been attracted to the large numbers of water birds which must have been around. He probably attacked them on the water with throwing sticks, or by running them down during the moult, and of course their eggs were a valuable source of protein.

Gathering, as opposed to hunting, has always been an important source of food principally in the warmer regions, and during suitable seasons the possibilities were almost inexhaustible with fruits, nuts, various roots, eggs, shell fish and honey as a small part of the total available to early Man.

When vegetable foods were in short supply, very likely the stomach content of the herbivores were eaten. Most of the gathering, judging from modern parallels, was done by the woman and young children and it was the women's job to prepare the skins and make the clothing. Curing of skins was made possible by using the brains of animals or urine, and scrapers were most likely used for working down the skins to make them supple. They were finished off by chewing, just as the Eskimo women used to do. For making the clothes, there were bone needles from the late Solutrean and bone awls from the earlier Upper Palaeolithic. The garments consisted of tunic, trousers and some form of hood, and there would have been some form of shoe or boot, though there are a number of prints of bare feet in the clay in some of the

French caves, suggesting that they went barefoot at times.

Combining all the available information from the European Upper Palaeolithic, we are able to build up a picture of settled communities living under far better conditions than was originally supposed. Their shelter was more than adequate; the mammoth houses of the south Russian plains must have been very snug. The food supply seems to have been more than sufficient, and the development of various forms of art in both eastern and western Europe suggests that Cro-Magnon Man had an advanced culture and a great deal of leisure time.

How large these prehistoric communities were can only be based on figures obtained from modern hunting groups. The basic unit was undoubtedly the family, and probably did not exceed about 10 to 12 individuals. Many hunting peoples seem to have had children only every four years and, infant mortality being high, the bands would never have been large. In view of the evidence regarding communal hunting, it is reasonable to suppose that several families joined together for drives. These would have been periods during which much gossip and information would have been exchanged, and marriages arranged.

While these comparisons with modern peoples must remain largely speculative the range of opportunities that each modern group has exploited in its search for food was well within the mental range of prehistoric Man and he had the equipment necessary to cope with most of the problems of survival, thus clearly raising his standard of living to well above the mere subsistence level and producing much the same solutions for the same kinds of problems faced even today by the small tribal groups living in isolated regions of the world.

Far left
South American Indian children playing a game with bows and arrows.

As with all hunting and fighting peoples, children were expected to be familiar with their equipment from a very early age and, as with modern children, they were encouraged to use the scaled down equipment of their elders. When the boys were young this equipment would have been used in play. This experience stood the potential hunter in good stead in later life when he was playing for real. Although most of the very young children would have accompanied the women gathering, when old enough to keep up with the men the boys would have been taken along on hunting trips.

Left
The Bushmen, like many peoples living in warm climates, depend more on gathering than on hunting. The digging stick must have been a universal tool for all food gathering—whether for roots, for digging small animals out of their burrows or breaking open termite nests.

The bushman digging stick was weighted with a bored stone, but this is a refinement, not an essential part. Some hunters also use a throwing stick for hitting ground birds, water birds or small game such as hares.

Below
North American Indians in wolf skins stalking bison (from a painting by Catlin). It is interesting that one predator, the Indian, should disguise himself as another, but the bison would have been more suspicious of Man than of the wolves.

With regard to the various forms of deception practised by hunters, adopting the quarries' movements is more important than a visual disguise and the Bushman hunters are very skilful at this form of imitation.

Previous pages
Bushman stalking a herd of wildebeest through the long grass. The Bushmen's main weapon was a small bow with poisoned arrows. Without the poison the bow would have been useless for large game as it was far too small and had a very limited range.

The poison made up by the Bushmen was derived both from plant sap and from snakes, spiders and a particular species of caterpillar. Some of these poisons, though effective, were not instantaneous and, after being hit, it was often necessary to follow the wounded animals for several days.

There is no direct evidence of the use of bows in the Upper Palaeolithic, still less that of poison. But if they were in use, much more powerful bows could have been employed, as there were far more suitable woods both for bows and arrows.

Left
Tasaday family in a cave in the Philippines. This must resemble many of the patterns of prehistoric families living in the tropics though not all of the hunting and gathering groups use caves to any extent. The Australians spend much of their time living in the open without any shelter, in spite of the intense cold at night and their total lack of clothing. The Bushmen seem to make more use of simple grass huts and wind breaks, but much of the earlier Bushman material is found in rock-shelters, which they used before being driven out of their original hunting grounds by the incoming cattle peoples from the north. In prehistoric Europe any form of shelter would have been at a premium, and even during the Interglacials the European climate would not have been warm enough all the year round to favour survival without early Man having some very adequate protection.

The problem of shelter is noticed in particular with the hunters on the eastern European plains who through lack of caves were forced to make very substantial huts, and the Eskimo igloo fulfils the same purpose.

Above
The Tasaday, only recently discovered, live completely on gathering with a diet consisting of vegetable foods, grubs, frogs and freshwater crabs. They live in caves, and possess very little equipment. Their method of making fire is based on the standard technique of rubbing two sticks, which is used all over the world.

The principle is simple: the longer stick is rotated in a shallow depression in the other, thus setting up sufficient friction to produce fire in the tinder which surrounds the base of the fire stick. Usually the rotating stick is of harder wood than the other, and of course both must be completely dry. Ideally two operators work the rotating stick, sliding their hands down as the stick is turned, and then the second operator takes the place of the first at the top of the stick so that the rotary motion is not interrupted.

The Eskimos, while adopting the same principle, use a small bow to produce the rotation. The components of these fire sticks are of course perishable and no prehistoric examples are known, but from some sites pyrites have been found suggesting the use of a flint and steel technique. Fire has been used at least since Peking Man, but there is no evidence as to how it was started.

Overleaf
In this case the tool held by a Tasaday is little more than a flat piece of stone hafted between a bent stick and is probably used as a simple hammer. In the tropical forests the equipment can be reduced to a minimum, spears need not be more than sharpened bamboo poles, which incidentally provide the blow gun. All the activities requiring cutting can be carried out with bamboo knives which can have a very sharp edge, though this is not very long lasting.

This brings us to the danger of trying to assess the mental capabilities of prehistoric peoples on the basis of their material culture alone. This becomes a matter not of capability, but of what equipment is required to adapt to which kind of environment. By comparison with their tropical contemporaries, the Magdalenians had a very sophisticated and complex culture, and without it they would never have survived in the environment in which they lived. The same applies to the Eskimos and the Bushmen, two highly intelligent peoples whose life-styles and equipment are totally different, and it is only in terms of their intellectual attainments that they can be judged.

Above
Eskimos making an ice storehouse. The Eskimos, like the Magdalenians long before them, have developed a sophisticated style of life which is completely attuned to the harsh environment in which they live. Eskimo dwellings and store-houses are constructed from the one natural resource which is truly abundant in their lands: ice. From the few animals and fish that they hunt, the Eskimos obtain all they need by way of meat, skins, sinews, and bones for needles and hooks.

Right
The shaman, like the medicine man whose function he shares, played a very important part among the Eskimos as well as the tribes in northern Siberia. Part-priest, part-physician and keeper of the tribal law and traditions, he was a member of the tribe with the responsibility for the continuity of tribal tradition. If Palaeolithic art did have a ritual function, then it would have been the shaman's duty to act as master of ceremonies, and it is possible that it was he who was responsible for much of the art itself. Was it the shaman who presided over the art school, making his pupils repeat their drawings on stone slabs over and over again? Was it he and his apprentices who carved the clay bison at Tuc d'Audoubert in the French Pyrenees in preparation for a forthcoming ritual? In the picture the shaman is fulfilling yet another role—that of story-teller and troubadour, accompanying his songs on a skin drum, to while away the long winter nights.

Index

ACKNOWLEDGMENTS

The publishers would like to thank the following individuals and organisations for their kind permission to reproduce the photographs in this book. All photographs, unless otherwise credited, were very kindly provided by the author.

British Museum (Natural History) 24 below right; J. Allan Cash Ltd. 84; Michael Day 32 below, 33 below; Nancy De Vore 13 above; Mary Evans Picture Library 9 above, 54; Claus Hansmann 74–5; Robert Harding Associates 23 above, (Wally Herbert Collection) 82–3; John Hillelson Agency (J. Nance/Magnum Distribution) 90, (Brian Seed) 87 above, 88–9; Alan Hutchison Library 34 below; Imitor Ltd. 31 above; Jacana Agence de Presse (Ph. Guy Bernard) 10–11, (J. Robert) 35 above; Mansell Collection 87 below; Guy Mary-Rousselière 94 above and below; Naturhistorisches Museum, Wien 75 above; Mark Newcomer 63 above; Photographie Giraudon (Lauros) 79 above left; Rapho Agence de Presse (Andujar) 86, (Camerapix) 27, (De Sazo) 50–1, (Michaud) 39 below; Snark International 73 below, 76–7; Tony Stone Associates 18–19; Transworld Feature Syndicate (UK) Ltd. (John Launois) 91, 92–3 and 80; United Kingdom Atomic Energy Authority 24 below left; ZEFA Picture Library (UK) Ltd. (Douglass Baglin) 71 below, 85, (Dr. Hans Kramarz) 81.

The publishers would also like to thank the following artists for supplying the illustrations.

David Nockels 1, 2–3, 4–5, 14–15, 36–7, 46–7, 52–3, 58–9, 68–9; Ralph Stobart 7 below, 9 below, 12 left, 13 below, 20, 22, 23 below, 24 above, 25, 28, 44 below, 57 below, 64 below, 67 inset; Asteris 49, (after l'Abbé Breuil) 71 above, 73 above, 75 below, 78.